The
Game
For
All
America

The Game For All America was made possible with the generous assistance of Fuji Photo·Film U.S.A., Inc., and Major League Baseball, which has assigned its royalties to the Baseball Alumni Team, a nonprofit foundation operated by and dedicated to helping former major leaguers.

This publication is a licensed product of Major League Baseball.

Published in the United States by THE SPORTING NEWS Publishing Co., 1212 North Lindbergh Boulevard, St. Louis, Missouri 63132.

Library of Congress Catalog Card Number: 88-60161

ISBN: 0-89204-279-6

10 9 8 7 6 5 4 3 2 1

First Edition

The
Game
For
All
America

Table of Contents

PREFACE

By Baseball Commissioner Peter V. Ueberroth

Congratulations to The Sporting News, Fuji Film and John Thorn for their extraordinary efforts in compiling *The Game For All America*. It is a compelling work that wonderfully illustrates every aspect of our national pastime, from morning until night, from one coast of America to the other.

There's something special about the game of baseball that allows its essence to be captured so well in print and through photographs. From the dreams and aspirations of youngsters in peewee leagues, to the dedication and kindness of stadium and concession stand operators, to the excitement and devotion of fans of all ages, to the confidence and power exhibited by the major leaguers, this book paints a complete picture of a sport that tugs at the conscience of America.

It reminds me of an extraordinary event that took place in a small village in upstate New York named Cooperstown not long ago. I was there for the Hall of Fame induction ceremony. The morning following the ceremony I left the hotel early, about six in the morning. Outside, I was surprised to find a line of people winding its way around the hotel, down a street toward the lake. I don't know how many were there, but they were all waiting patiently—no pushing, no shoving. When somebody wanted to get breakfast or grab a newspaper, those in line saved that person's spot.

I asked an elderly woman at the head of the line what they were doing there and she told me an autograph session was going to take place at 10 a.m., some four hours away.

I looked at the people in line. I saw

men and women. I saw little girls and 80-year-old men. I saw blacks, whites, hispanics, Asiatics. I saw prosperous looking people and others who appeared down on their luck.

What other profession, I thought, would draw this many people to an autograph session that featured men who hadn't taken an active part in their trade for more than 20 years? Certainly not politicians, or scientists, or businessmen, or even athletes from other sports.

But then baseball is much more than a profession. More than just a sport. It's a part of the fabric of our way of life, which is what this book is all about.

Acknowledgments

The title "The Game For All America" was borrowed from Detroit Tigers announcer Ernie Harwell's classic essay that first appeared on the pages of *The Sporting News* in 1955.

A special thank you to the following people who lent their generous assistance to this project: Sylvia Sutherland of the central region of the Little League; Larry Emerson and the staff at Spectrum Photo Services of St. Louis; Major League Baseball umpire Terry Tata, and all of the public relations directors of major league teams.

For my three sons, Jed, Isaac and Mark

The Game
For
All America

Baseball has been very, very good to us. It has given America rest and recreation, myths and memories, heroes and history. It has mirrored our society and sometimes propelled it, offering models for democracy, community, commerce and common humanity. And as our national game, baseball in no small measure defines us as Americans, enriching our language and imagery and connecting us with our countrymen in a grand tradition that crosses all barriers of generation, class, race and creed.

Baseball in America is more than a game, an observation to which this book is testimony and tribute. But it is first and foremost a game, a fact too often obscured amid today's talk of mega-dollar deals; and it is for the freedom—or rather, license—to play that an overly solemn America was first indebted to baseball. Before the wonderful photos that follow show what baseball means to us today, let's see how simple child's play came to be a national institution, and what bounties this great game has bestowed upon all America.

America Learns to Play

Even when baseball was in its infancy in the 1850s—having just evolved from the boyhood game of rounders and its more formalized derivative, town ball—the game already was shaping the life of the country. Americans of the previous generation were blind to the virtue of play (much to the befuddlement of laid-back Europeans) and permitted themselves few amusements that could not be justified in terms of social or business utility, or "seriousness." Nonconformists like the Olympic Town Ball Club of Philadelphia in the 1830s had to put up with a lot of guff, as this contemporary account details:

The first day that the Philadelphia men took the field . . . only four men were found to play, so they started in by playing a game called cat ball. All the players were over 25 years of age, and to see them playing a game like this caused much merriment among the friends of the players. It required "sand" in those days to go out on the field and play, as the prejudice against the game was very great. It took nearly a whole season to get men enough together to make a team, owing to the ridicule heaped upon the players for taking part in such childish sports.

What brought scorn upon the heads of these staunch

devotees of town ball (also known as "Boston Ball" or the "Massachusetts Game") was that although the game had regularly positioned fielders and demanded a modicum of strategic play, it still bore the childish essence of rounders: the retirement of a baserunner by throwing the ball at him, which necessitated a softer, less resilient ball than that used in the manly sport of cricket. What genius came up with the idea of putting out a runner by touching him with the ball or securing it "in the hands of an adversary on the base?" Probably Alexander Cartwright, who is known today as "the man who invented baseball," though it may have been D. L. Adams or William Wheaton or William Tucker. No matter—this was the first step toward making an American game that could challenge boys and men alike, and that could take its place in the life of a nation as cricket had in England. Henry Chadwick, the English-born cricket reporter who coined the term "national pastime" and became known as the "Father of Baseball," wrote that early on he:

. . . was struck with the idea that base ball was just the game for a national sport for Americans and . . . that from this game of ball a powerful lever might be made by which our people could be lifted into a position of more devotion to physical exercise and healthful outdoor recreation than they had, hitherto, been noted for. . . . In fact, as is well-known, we were the regular target for the shafts of raillery and even abuse from our outdoor-sport-loving cousins of England, in consequence of our national neglect of sports and pastimes, and our too great devotion to business and the "Almighty Dollar." But thanks to Base Ball . . . we have been transformed into quite another people. . . .

The transformation was from a hard-working but grim citizenry to a nation devoted to fresh air and exercise, not unlike the current rage for jogging, aerobics and weight-resistance training. Amateur baseball clubs sprang up like dandelions in the years immediately before the Civil War, but these were formed more for camaraderie and calisthenics than the pursuit of victory or the honing of skills. The demands of the new game on athleticism were few as the one-bound rule remained in effect (an out was recorded if a ball was caught on a bounce), and a couple of weeks' practice was enough to make a novice of 40 a creditable player. Men viewed baseball as a mild pastime, or relief from the mental strains of work; as a tonic, restorative of the physical energies needed for work; or a release of the surplus nervous energy that impedes young men in their pursuit of hard work. America in the mid-1850s was learning how to play, but still viewed sport in terms of its salutary effects on commerce; not until the close of the War Between the States would the focus shift to learning how to play well, for its own sake.

The Charm of the Game

Today we think of baseball as an anachronism, a last vestige of America's agrarian paradise—an idyllic game that takes us back to a more innocent time. But baseball originated in New York City, not rural Cooperstown, and in truth was an exercise in nostalgia from the beginning. Alexander Cartwright and his Knickerbockers began play in Madison Square in 1842, and the city's progress uptown soon compelled them to move up to Murray Hill. When the grounds there also were threatened by the march of industry, the Knicks ferried across the Hudson River to the Elysian Fields of Hoboken, a landscaped retreat of picnic grounds and scenic vistas that was designed by its proprietors to relieve New Yorkers of city air and city care.

In other words, the purpose of baseball's primal park was the same as that of New York's Central Park or, much later, Boston's Fenway Park—to give an increasingly urban populace a park within the city, a place reminiscent of the idealized farms that sent all these lads to the metropolis.

Thus the attraction of the game in its earliest days was first the novelty and exhilaration of play; second the opportunity for deskbound city clerks to expend surplus energy in a sylvan setting, freed from the tyranny of the clock; and third, to harmonize with an American golden age, almost entirely legendary.

Simple charms, simple pleasures. In the late 1860s, advancing skills led to heightened appetites for victory, which led to hot pursuit of the game's gifted players, which inevitably led to sub rosa payments and, by 1870, rampant professionalism. The gentlemanly players of baseball's first generation retreated from the field, shaking their heads in dismay at how greed had perverted the "grand old game"—now barely a score of years old—and probably ruined it forever.

Sound familiar? It should—the same dire and premature announcements of the demise of the game have been issued ever since, spurred by free-agent signings, long-term contracts, no-trade provisions, integration, night ball, rival leagues, ad infinitum. The only conclusions a calm head could draw from this recurring cycle of contempt for the present and glorification of the past are that (a) things ain't what they used to be and never were; (b) fully accurate assessment of a present predicament is impossible, for it requires perspective; and (c) no matter what the owners or players or rulesmakers or fans do, they can't kill baseball. All three conclusions are correct. In baseball, the distinction between amateur and professional is not clear-cut: an amateur may play for devotion to the game, *amat* being Latin for love, but a professional does not play for pursuit of gain alone; he plays for love, too.

Oh, don't you remember the game of base-ball we saw twenty
* years ago played,*
When contests were true, and the sight free to all, and
* home-runs in plenty were made?*
When we lay on the grass, and with thrills of delight,
* watched the ball squarely pitched at the bat,*
And easily hit, and then mount out of sight along with our
* cheers and our hat?*
And then, while the fielders raced after the ball, the men on
* the bases flew round,*
And came in together—four batters in all. Ah! That was
* the old game renowned.*
Now salaried pitchers, who throw the ball curved at padded
* and masked catchers lame*
And gate-money music and seats all reserved is all that is
* left of the game.*
Oh, give us the glorious matches of old, when love of true sport
* made them great,*
And not this new-fashioned affair always sold for the boodle
* they take at the gate.*

—*H. C. Dodge*

That doomsday ditty was published in the year *The Sporting News* was founded, 1886.

The National Pastime

America before the Civil War was still populated by a handful of veterans of the Revolutionary War and many who remembered vividly the War of 1812. The era of Anglo-American amity had not yet dawned; our country's spiritual separation from the Mother Country, begun in

1776 and legally confirmed in 1783, was still in progress. And having baseball to rival and replace cricket was an important step in that process. Moreover, when England, seeking to maintain its supply of cotton from the American South, appeared over-cordial to the Confederate cause, anti-British feeling swept the North. An America long suffering from an inferiority complex toward England now turned against cricket and embraced baseball with increased fervor.

From 1856 on, Henry Chadwick had been eager for baseball to rise to the status in America that cricket held in his native England. He championed the game tirelessly, helping to refine its rules and practices to make it the equal of cricket as a "manly" and "scientific" game. And baseball soon became, in his words, like cricket "a game requiring the mental powers of judgment, calculation and quick perception to excel in it—while in its demands upon the vigor, endurance and courage of manhood, its requirements excel those requisite to become equally expert as a cricketer."

Chadwick invented a method of scorekeeping and statistical compilation patterned on those which were inaugurated in cricket. Baseball was an elemental game—pitch, hit, catch, throw—like other games of ball; but keeping records of the contests and later printing box scores and individual averages elevated it from rounders and placed it on an equal footing with its transatlantic cousin. As important, the records served to legitimize men's concern with what had been merely a boys' exercise by making it more "serious," like the numerically annotated world of business. Today, baseball without records is inconceivable: They are what keep Babe Ruth and Ty Cobb and Walter Johnson alive in our minds in a way that President James K. Polk, Walter Reed or Admiral

Dewey—arguably greater men—are not.

By the end of the Civil War, cricket in this country remained a pastime for a shrinking band of Anglophiles, while the New York Game of Baseball (as it was then called to differentiate it from the nearly vanished Massachusetts Game) was spreading across the country, courtesy of returning veterans whose first exposure to baseball might have come in a prisoner-of-war camp. In the press, baseball was typically proclaimed The National Game—the same term Britons used for cricket.

Play for Pay

From its creation in 1871 to its crash five years later, the National Association had a rocky time as America's first professional league. Franchises came and went with dizzying speed, often folding in midseason. Schedules were not played out if a club slated to go on the road saw little prospect of gain. Drinking and gambling and game-fixing were rife. And the Boston Red Stockings of Al Spalding and the Wright brothers dominated play, going 71-8 in the last of their four straight championship seasons; their predictable and one-sided victories crushed the competition and, at last, interest in the entire circuit.

But from the ashes of the National Association emerged the Red Stockings' model of success and the entrepreneurial genius of Chicago's William Hulbert. After raiding Boston to obtain four of the biggest stars in the game—Spalding, Ross Barnes, Deacon White and Cal McVey—and lining up the services of the Philadelphia Athletics' Adrian Anson, the White Stockings were ready to roll in the National League of Professional Base Ball Clubs, founded on February 2, 1876, in New York's Grand Central Hotel.

The first five years of the N.L. were nearly as unsettled

as the final years of the N.A., with franchises appearing and then disappearing in such cities as Syracuse, Troy, Worcester and Hartford while major cities like New York and Philadelphia were, after the league's inaugural year, unrepresented. In 1878, the fledgling circuit was forced to cut back to six teams: Milwaukee, Indianapolis, Chicago, Providence, Cincinnati and Boston. *National* League? *National* Game? It seemed Americans had plenty of appetite for playing the game, but not much for watching it.

Yet as the National League suffered with growing pains, it was introducing some elements that were critical to the explosion of interest that came with the 1880s. It created a professional (paid) umpiring crew; insisted that the league schedule be honored; banned pool selling and hard-liquor consumption in the stands, and created a system of management-owned teams as opposed to the player-run cooperatives that largely characterized the N.A. As the public's renewed faith in the integrity of the game coincided with an upswing in the national economy, not only the National League flourished—an interloper, the rival American Association, came along to offer patrons 25-cent baseball (N.L. admissions were 50 cents), Sunday games and beer. With the public's new appetite for the game seeming insatiable, a group of investors led by St. Louis' Henry Lucas founded a *third* major league, the Union Association, in 1884.

With brash stars like Cap Anson, Tim Keefe, Dan Brouthers and the larger-than-life King Kelly capturing the newspaper headlines and the nation's imagination, the age of the baseball idol arrived. Before this decade, men like Jim Creighton, Joe Start and George Wright were admired in New York and New England, but now a baseball hero's image could be mass-produced for nationwide sale, or

licensed for advertising, or inspire odes and songs. Kelly inspired *Slide, Kelly, Slide,* its arcane references now largely forgotten but once the most popular song in the land:

> *Slide, Kelly, slide!*
> *Your running's a disgrace!*
> *Slide, Kelly, slide!*
> *Stay there, hold your base!*
> *If someone doesn't steal ya,*
> *And your batting doesn't fail ya,*
> *They'll take you to Australia!*
> *Slide, Kelly, slide!*

And although its author, Ernest Lawrence Thayer, always denied it, Kelly could well have been the model for the immortal lyric ballad, "Casey at the Bat," now in its hundredth year and still going strong.

Baseball was ascendant in the 1880s and, like the budding nation whose pastime it was, pretty cocksure of itself. In the same summer that "Casey" made his debut, 1888, Albert Spalding led a contingent of baseball players on a round-the-world tour, spreading the gospel of bat and ball to such places as Egypt, Italy, England, Hawaii and the above-mentioned Australia. Baseball, America thought, was too grand a game to be merely a national pastime; it ought to be the international pastime.

At a New York banquet for Spalding's returning "world tourists" in 1889, speaker Mark Twain declared, "Baseball is the very symbol, the outward and visible expression of the drive and push and rush and struggle of the raging, tearing, booming nineteenth century." Spalding himself later wrote:

I claim that Base Ball owes its prestige as our National

*Game to the fact that as no other form of sport it is the
exponent of American Courage, Confidence, Combativeness;
American Dash, Discipline, Determination; American
Energy, Eagerness, Enthusiasm; American Pluck, Persistency,
Performance; American Spirit, Sagacity, Success; American
Vim, Vigor, Virility.*

In fact baseball had become more than the mere
reflection of our rising industrial and political power and its
propensity for bluster and hokum: the national game was
beginning to *supply* models for democracy, industry and
community that would change America and the world—not
in the ways that Spalding's tourists may have envisioned,
but indisputably for the better.

A Model Institution

Father Chadwick had been typically prescient when he
wrote in 1876, the inaugural year of major league play and
the centenary of America's birth:

*What Cricket is to an Englishman, Base-Ball has become to
an American. . . . On the Cricket-field—and there only—the
Peer and the Peasant meet on equal terms; the possession of
courage, nerve, judgment, skill, endurance and activity alone
giving the palm of superiority. In fact, a more democratic
institution does not exist in Europe than this self-same
Cricket; and as regards its popularity, the records of the
thousands of Commoners, Divines and Lawyers, Legislators
and Artisans, and Literateurs as well as Mechanics and
Laborers, show how great a hold it has on the people. If this
is the characteristic of Cricket in aristocratic and
monarchical England, how much more will the same
characteristics mark Base-Ball in democratic and
republican America.*

Chadwick's vision of baseball as a model democratic
institution would have to wait for the turn of the century to
be fully articulated, and for Jackie Robinson and Branch
Rickey to be fully realized. But Chadwick's belief that
baseball could be more than a game, could become a
model of and for American life, presaged baseball's golden
age of 1903-30.

The tumultuous 1890s witnessed a player revolt against
high-handed and monopolistic management, followed by a
nearly ruinous contraction from three major leagues to one
12-team circuit. The national economy suffered a panic in
1893 and a sluggish recovery thereafter; baseball attendance
dwindled; and the lack of a World Series after 1890 was
sorely felt. The game was in a period of consolidation, or
hibernation, or stagnation, your perspective depending upon
whether you were an owner, fan or player.

But then Ban Johnson came along, fired by the same
vision of a rival league that had inflamed the Players League
and the American and Union Associations before him, and
that would beckon to the Federal and Continental Leagues
later on. With the establishment of the American League
and the signing of a peace treaty with the Nationals in 1903,
the World Series was resumed, prosperity returned and the
popularity and influence of the game exploded.

Baseball mania seized America as new heroes like
Christy Mathewson, Honus Wagner, Ty Cobb, Walter
Johnson and Nap Lajoie found a public hungry for
knowledge of their every action, their every thought. A
fan's affiliation with his team could exceed in vigor his
attachment to his church, his trade, his political party—all
but family and country, and even these were wrapped up in
baseball. The national pastime became the great repository
of national ideals, the symbol of all that was good in
American life: fair play (sportsmanship), the rule of law

(objective arbitration of disputes), equal opportunity (each side has its innings), the brotherhood of man (bleacher harmony), and more.

The baseball boom of the early 20th century built on the game's simple charms of exercise and communal celebration, adding the psychological and social complexities of vicarious play: civic pride, role models and hero worship. It became routine for the President to throw out the first ball of the season. Supreme Court Justices had inning-by-inning scores from the World Series relayed to their chambers. Business leaders, perhaps disingenuously, praised baseball as a model of competition and fair play. "Baseball," opined a writer for *American Magazine* in 1913, "has given our public a fine lesson in commercial morals. . . . Some day all business will be reorganized and conducted by baseball standards."

Leaders of recent immigrants advised their peoples to learn the national game if they wanted to become Americans, and foreign-language newspapers devoted space to educating their readers about America's strange and wonderful game. (New York's *Staats-Zeitung,* for example, applauded *Kraftiges Schlagen*—hard hitting—and cautioned German fans not to kill the *Unparteiischer.*) As historian Harold Seymour wrote, "The argot of baseball supplied a common means of communication and strengthened the bond which the game helped to establish among those sorely in need of it—the mass of urban dwellers and immigrants living in the anonymity and impersonal vortex of large industrial cities. . . . With the loss of the traditional ties known in a rural society, baseball gave to many the feeling of belonging." And rooting for a baseball team permitted city folk, newcomers and native born, the sense of pride in community that in former times, when they lived in small towns, was commonplace.

Thus baseball offered a model of how to be an American, to be part of the team. Baseball was "second only to death as a leveler," wrote Allen Sangree. Even in those horrifically leveling years of 1941-45, when so many of our bravest and brightest gave their lives to defend American ideals, baseball's role as a vital enterprise was confirmed by President Franklin Delano Roosevelt's "green light" for continued play. Many of baseball's best players—Ted Williams, Joe DiMaggio, Hank Greenberg and Bob Feller, to name a few—swapped their baseball gear for Uncle Sam's, and served with military distinction or helped to boost the nation's morale. Even oldtimers like Babe Ruth, Walter Johnson and Ty Cobb donned uniforms in service of their country—baseball uniforms, as they staged exhibitions on behalf of war bonds. Servicemen overseas looked to letters from home and the box scores in *The Sporting News* to keep them in touch with what they had left behind, and what they were fighting for—an American way of life that was a beacon for a world in which the light of freedom had been nearly extinguished.

If you will indulge a personal aside, I was one of the countless immigrants who from the 1860s on saw baseball as the "open sesame" to the door of their adopted land. A Polish Jew born in occupied Germany to Holocaust survivors—on Alexander Cartwright's birthday, I later learned—I arrived on these shores at age 2. After checking in at Ellis Island, I happened by chance to spend the first night in my new land in the no-longer-elegant hotel where in 1876 the National League had been founded. I learned to read by studying the backs of Bowman baseball cards, and to be an American by attaching myself passionately to the Brooklyn Dodgers (who also taught me about the fickleness of love).

The Brooklyn Dodgers, in the persons particularly of

Rickey and Robinson, also taught America a lesson: that baseball's integrative and democratic models, by the 1940s long held to be verities, were hollow at the core. David Halberstam has written:

. . . it was part of our folklore, basic to our national democratic myth, that sports was the great American equalizer, that money and social status did not matter upon the playing fields. Elsewhere life was assumed to be unfair: those who had privilege passed it on to their children, who in turn had easier, softer lives. Those without privilege were doomed to accept the essential injustices of daily life. But according to the American myth, in sports the poor but honest kid from across the tracks could gain (often in competition with richer, snottier kids) recognition and acclaim for his talents.

Until October 23, 1945, when Robinson signed a contract to play for the Montreal Royals, Brooklyn's top farm club, the myth as far as blacks were concerned was not a sustaining legend, but a mere falsehood.

Rickey's rectitude and Robinson's courage have become central legends of baseball and America, exemplars of decency and strength that inspire all of us. Their "great experiment" came too late for such heroes of black ball as Josh Gibson, Oscar Charleston and Ray Dandridge, but its success has been complete. Once the integrative or leveling model of baseball—all America playing and working in harmony—was extended to blacks, the effect on the nation was profound. Eighty years after the Civil War, America had proved itself unable to practice the values for which it was fought, so baseball showed the way. This is what Commissioner Ford Frick said to the St. Louis Cardinals, rumored to be planning a strike in May 1947:

If you do this you will be suspended from the league. You will find that the friends you think you have in the press box will not support you, that you will be outcasts. I do not care if half the league strikes. Those who do it will encounter quick retribution. They will be suspended and I don't care if it wrecks the National League for five years. This is the United States of America, and one citizen has as much right to play as any other. The National League will go down the line with Robinson whatever the consequence.

As Monte Irvin said, "Baseball has done more to move America in the right direction than all the professional patriots with their billions of cheap words." The Supreme Court decision of *Brown vs. Topeka Board of Education;* civil rights heroes like Martin Luther King, James Meredith, Thurgood Marshall and others; the freedom marches and the voting rights act—all were vital to America's progress toward unity, but the title of one of Jackie Robinson's books may not overstate the case: *Baseball Has Done It.*

A final way in which baseball supplies models for America is one that has been present from the game's beginning: a model for boys wishing to be men, wrestling with their insecurities and wondering, *What does it mean to be a man? What does a man do?* The answers in baseball, at least, are unequivocal; as Satchel Paige said in his later years, "I loved baseball. There wasn't no 'maybe so' about it."

Baseball gives boys (and girls) a sense of how wide the world is, in its possibilities as well as its geography. Reading the summations of minor-league ball in *The Sporting News* each week piqued the curiosity of baseball-mad boys like me. Where were Kokomo, Mattoon, Thibodeaux and Nogales? What did people look like in Salinas or Rocky Mount? What did they do in

Artesia? How many exciting, exotic places this enormous country contained! But a note of comfort—they couldn't be all that strange, could they, if baseball was played there.

And to that other vast *terra incognita*—the world of adults—baseball also offered a road map. How many boys learned to talk with grown-ups, principally their fathers, by nodding wisely at an assessment of a shortstop's range or a pitcher's heart, and mock-confidently venturing an opinion about the hometown team's chances? Our dads are our first heroes (and, decades later, our last); but in between, baseball players are what we want to be. For heroes are larger than life, and when as adults we have taken a measure of ourselves and found we are no more than life-size, it can be fortifying to puff ourselves up now and then. Douglass Wallop put it nicely:

. . . only yesterday the fan was a kid of nine or ten bolting his breakfast on Saturday morning and hurtling from the house with a glove buttoned over his belt and a bat over his shoulder, rushing to the nearest vacant lot, perhaps the nearest alley, where the other guys were gathering, a place where it would always be spring. For him, baseball would always have the sound and look and smell of that morning and of other mornings just like it. Only by an accident of chance would he find himself, in the years to come, up in the grandstand, looking on. But for a quirk of fate, he himself would be down on that field; it would be his likeness on the television screen and his name in the newspaper high on the list of .300 hitters. He was a fan, but a fan only incidentally. He was, first and always, himself a baseball player.

The Fifties

If the America that was survives anywhere as more than a memory, it is in baseball, that strangely pastoral game in no matter what setting—domed stadium or Little League field. As hindsight improves upon foresight, memory improves upon reality, so that the endless monotony and grinding physical labor of small-town life before the Civil War are now thought quite romantic. I may be in a distinct minority, but I am not alone in the opinion that life in today's urban, technological, contentious, debt-ridden America is by and large better than it ever was.

I venture to say there are more folks—though by no means a majority—who would believe the same about baseball. Today's players are better than those in the game's golden age, heroes like Ruth and Gehrig excepted; the strategy of the game and even its execution are more adept and the opportunities to watch it, if not to play it, far exceed those of say, the 1950s, which today is broadly regarded as the game's halcyon era. (A golden age may be defined flexibly, it seems, so as to coincide with the period of one's youth.) For all its pull toward the good old days, for all its statistical illusions of an Olympian era when titans strode the basepaths, for all its seeming permanence in a world aswirl with change, baseball has in fact moved with America into a new age more golden than any before.

The period after World War II was a heady time for the nation and its pastime, both of them buoyed by returning veterans and removed restrictions. But in 1946 the major leagues still represented only the 16 cities that had participated in the National Agreement of 1903, none west of St. Louis; a handful of blacks were just entering the minor leagues after a half-century of exclusion, and because television was not yet a staple of the American home, most baseball fans had never seen *even a single* big-league game.

Women had been courted as patrons (even nonpaying patrons) ever since the game's dawn. Baseball management hoped that their presence would lend "tone" to the proceedings and keep a lid on the rowdies, in the stands and on the field. But women's participation in the game's labor force and management was even more limited than their role in the nation's business and industry—Rosie the Riveter and Eleanor Roosevelt as yet had no counterparts in baseball.

On the amateur level, while American Legion Junior Baseball had begun as early as 1928, and Little League in 1939, neither attained their heights until after the War ended. Nay sayers will point out that baseball has lost ground as more kids today play football, basketball, soccer and tennis than 50 years ago; but far more play baseball, too, and not only in America. The annual pursuit of the Little League championship in Williamsport, Pa. (like the Pan-American Games), has become an international affair, an instrument of diplomacy that State Department officials envy. Indeed, baseball may yet hold the key to restoring neighborly relations with Nicaragua and Cuba.

Baseball in the colleges, now so vibrant and so fertile with major league talent, was on the path to extinction by the end of the War, only to be brought back from the brink by the G.I. Bill. The explosive growth in enrollment the returning veterans produced also created a sudden need for expanded athletic programs, and baseball was the prime beneficiary. The NCAA's introduction of the College World Series in 1947 affirmed the game's recovery on campus, and since locating in Omaha three years later it has grown steadily.

In 1951, major league baseball, as dated from the inception of the National League in 1876, reached the august age of 75 and proclaimed its "diamond jubilee." Celebratory banquets were held, a plaque was erected at the old hotel where the league was founded and all N.L. players wore commemorative patches on their sleeves. Coincidentally but less flashily, the American League celebrated its 50th birthday that same year.

There was no question that baseball was booming at this point. On the professional level, a whopping 59 leagues contained 448 teams employing about 8,000 players—or roughly 19 minor leaguers competing for each of the then 400 spots in the big show. Little League would soon send its first alumnus to the majors, which had already accepted hundreds of graduates from Legion and other programs. Happy Chandler secured from television a then mind-boggling (but now, to network moguls, nostalgic) $6 million for broadcast rights to the next six World Series. And with the game's most powerful teams bunched in New York City—the Yankees, the Dodgers and the Giants—the publicity mills and the turnstiles were spinning as they had never spun before.

But the excitement of the first five postwar years was not confined to New York. Even such perennial tailenders as the Boston Braves, the Philadelphia Phillies and the Cleveland Indians fought their way into the World Series; and staid old Cleveland, under Bill Veeck's carnival-like direction, set staggering new attendance records. Many of the newly admitted black players had become stars and—satisfyingly, though few but Branch Rickey had predicted it—box-office attractions: Jackie Robinson, Roy Campanella and Don Newcombe of the Dodgers; Monte Irvin and rookie Willie Mays of the Giants; Sam Jethroe of the Braves; Larry Doby and Satchel Paige of the Indians. And many prewar and wartime stars continued to shine, like Bob Feller, Stan Musial and Ted Williams, while new ones like Gotham's center-field trio of Duke Snider, Mickey Mantle and Mays replenished the stock as heroes like Joe DiMaggio hung up their spikes.

But most of these blessings had their downside. Opening the game to black Americans was indubitably right, but it killed the Negro Leagues, ruining owners and abruptly ending many playing careers. The increasing organization of youth baseball, particularly the rise of the Little League, heightened the stress of baseball at its formative levels and drained much of the fun, as driven parents began to see their Junior as tomorrow's big leaguer, not as just a boy having fun while learning a thing or two. (Fortunately, the competitive excesses of the 1950s taught their own lesson: that baseball is for everyone.)

The game on the field was dominated by the home run, making for a brand of ball that might be termed dull. League leaders registered such stolen-base totals as Dom DiMaggio's 15 or Jackie Jensen's 22; Early Wynn led the A.L. in earned-run average one year with a 3.20 mark; and the three-base hit, despite the big old parks still prevalent, emulated the dodo. The pennant domination by the three New York teams—principally the Yankees, of course—made the national pastime a rather parochial pleasure; it was hard for fans in St. Louis or Detroit to wax rhapsodic over a Subway Series. No, the blessings of the 1950s were not unmitigated, any more than on the national scene the tranquility of the Eisenhower years were without cost.

Take television, for instance: The revenues were great, and so was the publicity value of electronically extending major league play to people in southern and western areas. But the novelty of big-time heroes on the small screen kept those folks at home when formerly they had gone to the local ball park. The minors began their long decline, one that didn't bottom out until 1964; by then the 59 leagues of 1951 had become 19, and the 8,000-odd professional players had dwindled to fewer than 2,500.

Moreover, television whetted the baseball appetites of Californians, Texans, Georgians, Washingtonians and more. That demand plus the development of faster passenger planes gave ideas to owners of two of baseball's decaying franchises. Walter O'Malley, owner of the Brooklyn Dodgers, and Giants' Owner Horace Stoneham had seen the solidarity of the original 16-city composition broken in 1953, when the venerable Boston Braves, a franchise established in the first year of the National Association, 1871, became the darlings of Milwaukee, and further weakened by the defections in 1954-55 of the St. Louis Browns to Baltimore and the Philadelphia Athletics to Kansas City. Amid weeping and gnashing of teeth that continue to this day, the Dodgers and Giants left for the Golden West in 1958.

In a strange twist, the architect of the move, O'Malley, was (and in the East, still is) widely seen as the snake in baseball's version of the Garden of Eden, responsible for ending the grand old game's paradisiacal age. Yet the placement of franchises in California, as distressing as it was for Brooklyn and Manhattan and as roundly condemned as it was by traditionalists, may now be seen as the best thing to happen to baseball in the decade. And Walter O'Malley, if you will permit your mind a considerable stretch, may be viewed not as the snake offering baseball the mortal apple; but as a latter-day Johnny Appleseed (in the footsteps of Alexander Cartwright, who in 1849 also headed for California in pursuit of gold yet is remembered not for his venality, but for bringing The New York Game to the West).

It was imperative that baseball take the game to where the people were, precisely as it had in 1903. America's population had already begun the westward and southward shift that was to become so pronounced in the 1960s and

'70s. The move to Los Angeles and San Francisco, rather than confirming those cities' stature as "big-league," as is so often written, brought baseball into step with America, which had long recognized them as such. Baseball could now call itself the national pastime without apology.

The Sixties

A chaotic decade for our country, the 1960s were worrisome, stormy years for baseball as well, with dramatic changes in league composition, playing styles, competitive balance and, most distressingly, the game's appeal to the American people. Baseball endured its ordeal by fire, and came through strengthened, though not unscathed.

The departure of the Dodgers and Giants in 1958 created a vacuum in New York and an increased hunger for baseball in new boomtowns like Houston, Atlanta and Minneapolis. Enter Branch Rickey, nearly 80 but still possessed of a keen nose for new opportunity. The great innovator who already had brought baseball the farm system and integration now created the Continental League, a paper league with paper franchises. Nonetheless, Rickey's mirage frightened Organized Baseball, remembering its ruinous fight with the Federal League of 1914-15, into expansion.

Two of the Continental "franchises"—the future New York Mets and Houston Colt .45s—were admitted for 1962. At the same time, the American League was authorized to commence its western foray one year earlier with the expansion-draft Los Angeles Angels and the relocated Minnesota Twins (the latter being the transplanted Washington Senators, who were replaced in the nation's capital by an ill-fated expansion team).

Other franchise shifts and startups in the decade had baseball's original vagabonds, the Milwaukee Braves by way of Boston, moving to Atlanta in 1966 and the erstwhile Athletics of Philadelphia, having failed in Kansas City, directing their caravan toward Oakland in 1968.

The A's were quickly replaced in K.C. by the Royals, one of two new teams introduced in each league with the expansion of 1969. This in turn precipitated divisional play and the League Championship Series, both inventions much decried at the time but now generally applauded. And in one of baseball's more forgettable debacles, the expansion Pilots of 1969 lost their course in Seattle after only one year and ran aground in Milwaukee, where they were rechristened the Brewers. The National League's expansion into San Diego and Montreal proceeded more smoothly, although Padres' attendance lagged behind expectations and the Expos' Olympic Stadium (replacing the stopgap Jarry Park) took longer to get its dome than Michelangelo took to paint St. Peter's.

On the field, the big-bang game of the 1950s was giving way to a pitching-and-defense formula, at least in the National League, which began to outstrip its long-time tormentor at the box office and in World Series and All-Star confrontations. Speed returned to the equation, too, as personified by first Maury Wills, and then Lou Brock (though both were preceded in the A.L. by Luis Aparicio). And a revolution in baseball strategy was brewing, as the 1959 success of such relievers as Larry Sherry, Lindy McDaniel and Roy Face paved the way for the universal adoption of the bullpen stopper in the 1960s.

In the American League expansion year of 1961, the first played to a 162-game schedule, the Bronx Bombers hit a prodigious 240 homers. Sluggers Harmon Killebrew, Norm Cash and Rocky Colavito all hit more than 40 and Mickey Mantle hit more than 50. These totals were troubling to Commissioner Ford Frick, but nowhere near as consternating as the 61 homers struck by Roger Maris to top the game's most famous record, the 60 that Babe Ruth walloped in 1927. After seeing the National League's scoring increase in 1962, its first year of expansion, Frick became concerned that pitchers were becoming an endangered species. He said:

I would even like the spitball to come back. Take a look at the batting, home run and slugging record for recent seasons, and you become convinced that the pitchers need help urgently.

Disastrously, Frick convinced the owners to widen the strike zone for 1963 to its pre-1950 dimensions: top of the shoulder to bottom of the knee. The result was to increase strikeouts, reduce walks and shrink batting averages within five years to levels unseen since 1908, the nadir of the deadball era. The once-proud Yankees, who had continued their long domination of the American League to mid-decade, saw their team batting average sink to an incredible .214 in 1968. That year produced an overall A.L. mark of .230 and a batting champion, Carl Yastrzemski, with an average of .301.

As pitchers vanquished batters, seemingly for all eternity, the bottom line was that the fans stayed away in droves. Attendance in the National League, which in 1966 reached 15 million, fell by 1968 to only 11.7 million. In fact, despite the addition of four new clubs in 1961-62, attendance in 1968 was only 3 million more than it had been in 1960. Critics charged that baseball was a geriatric vestige of an America that had vanished, a game too slow for a nation that was rushing toward the moon; its decline would only steepen, they claimed, as that more with-it national pastime, pro football, extended its mastery of the airwaves.

But the sky was not falling, despite the alarms of the chicken-lickens. The owners acted quickly to redress the game's balance between offense and defense, reducing the strike zone and lowering the pitcher's mound. But the most important change may have been one that was introduced in 1965 and was only beginning to take effect: the amateur free-agent draft. Typically successful teams like the Yankees, Dodgers, Braves and Cardinals had stayed successful because of their attention to scouting. Consistently they were able to garner more top prospects for their farm systems than clubs with less deep pockets or more volatile management. Now, teams that had fallen on hard times need not look toward a generation of famine before returning to the feast. Now, dynasties—awe-inspiring but not healthy for the game—were suddenly rendered implausible. Now, baseball had a competitive balance that could produce a rotation of electrifying successes among the leagues' cities, like the ascension of the Boston Red Sox from ninth place in 1966 to the pennant the next, and the amazing rise of the New York Mets from the netherworld to a world championship in 1969. The game would still have some hard rows to hoe in the 1970s, but there was no mistaking the reversal of its downturn: In the new age of "relevance," baseball was back.

The Seventies

The 1970s saw a continuation of the trend toward new stadium construction that had marked the 1960s and may well have triggered that decade's batting drought, as hitter's havens like Ebbets Field, the Polo Grounds and Sportsman's Park fell to the wrecker's ball. The 1960s had brought new ball parks to nine cities—San Francisco, Los Angeles, New York (N.L.), Houston, Atlanta, Anaheim, St. Louis, Oakland and San Diego. In 1970-71, baseball bade farewell to old friends Crosley Field, Forbes Field and Shibe Park as new stadiums—artificial-turf clones of each other—sprang up in Cincinnati, Pittsburgh and Philadelphia. Other new parks were built in Arlington, Kansas City, Montreal, Seattle and Toronto (the latter two, expansion franchises added to the American League in 1977), and Yankee Stadium underwent a massive facelift.

All this construction activity seemed to bespeak the game's profitability. Indeed, attendance was climbing in almost all major league cities, as heroes like Henry Aaron, Johnny Bench, Reggie Jackson and Pete Rose, to name but a few, gave the fans plenty to cheer about. And the controversial adoption of the designated hitter innovation by the American League in 1973 gave a further boost to hitting while giving fans much to argue about, which after all is one of baseball's great pleasures.

But the game's financial health was imperiled by rising player unrest and owner intransigence over labor issues, centered on the reserve clause which bound a player to his team in perpetuity while denying him the opportunity to gauge his worth in the free market. The reformulation of the relationship between players and management became the hallmark of the decade and sorely tested fans' devotion to the game.

It began with the momentous case brought against Organized Baseball by veteran outfielder Curt Flood in 1970, challenging the legality of the reserve clause. "I am a man," Flood said, "not a consignment of goods to be bought and sold." The Supreme Court ruled against Flood the following year, but the tenor for the 1970s had been set. A 13-day player strike delayed the opening of the 1972 season, and arbitrator Peter Seitz ruled the following year (in what has come to be known as the Messersmith-McNally case) that a player could establish his right of free agency by playing out his option year without a signed contract. The writing on the wall was clear: Free agency was

the wave of the future.

Big-name players like Jim Hunter, Reggie Jackson and Rich Gossage migrated to New York and lesser lights like Wayne Garland and Oscar Gamble signed elsewhere for figures that seemed incredible. In the race to sign available talent some owners spun out of control while others like Minnesota's Cal Griffith, without corporate coffers behind them, had no choice but to sit on the sideline. Player movement among stars jeopardized fan allegiances, pundits alleged, as Gossage and Jackson played for three teams in three years and championship teams like the Oakland A's and Boston Red Sox were broken up through trades that were forced by the specter of impending—and uncompensated—free-agent departures.

(Comfortingly to the historian, all this hubbub had occurred in very much the same way in 1869-70, before the advent of the reserve clause, when Henry Chadwick was fulminating about the perniciousness of players "revolving" from one team to another simply to advance their fortunes. Also, baseball's first avowedly professional team, Harry Wright's Cincinnati Red Stockings of 1869-70, were roundly abused for constructing their powerhouse team with "mercenaries" from other states—thus scorning baseball's core appeal to civic pride. Did New York's George Steinbrenner know the prestigious pedigree of his free-spending ways?)

What actually compromised fan loyalties in the '70s was not player movement—it took Yankee fans, oh, maybe, 10 minutes to regard Reggie as a born pinstriper—but player salaries. When the major league minimum was under $5,000 or so and only a Mantle, Williams, Musial or DiMaggio made $100,000 a year, fans saw their heroes as, by and large, working colleagues who had the supreme luck to play ball for a living. If a star made a splendiferous

THE GAME FOR ALL AMERICA

salary, that was socially useful as a model that any worker could make it big if he only had enough ability to emerge from the pack. But when stars began routinely to command seven-figure salaries, and more importantly the annual wage of the average major leaguer rose to six-figure levels, many adult breadwinners struggled to remain fans.

That they succeeded is testament to their love of the game, for fans have had a difficult assignment in reshaping their views of baseball players along the lines of media stars. The princely compensations of actors and pop musicians have long been accepted by the public as the verdict of the marketplace. If the movie *The Godfather* makes hundreds of millions of dollars for its studio and distributor, then Marlon Brando's multi-million-dollar fee for the film seems not out of line. Analogously, if the Dodgers are fabulously lucrative for ownership, then a lofty salary for Fernando Valenzuela does not now give rise to resentment among the fans. This sort of re-education is by no means complete, but barroom banter about baseball these days is not as bitterly one-note about "greedy players" as it was 10 years ago.

And you don't hear a peep about pro football replacing baseball as the national game.

The Eighties

The game on the field in the 1970s had been marked by an unprecedented commingling of power and speed; the great teams of Cincinnati, Baltimore and Oakland; the return to prominence of the Yankees, and the historic exploits of Henry Aaron and Pete Rose. The game in the '80s would begin with the Philadelphia Phillies, led by free-agent Rose and future Hall of Famers Mike Schmidt and Steve Carlton, ridding themselves of a historic stain. Until their victory over the Kansas City Royals, the Phils

were the only one of the original 16 major league franchises never to have won a World Series (the St. Louis Browns had to accept the help of their modern incarnation, the Baltimore Orioles).

The next year brought baseball's darkest moment since the Brotherhood revolt and ensuing Players League of 1890, as major league players walked off their jobs at the height of the season and didn't return for 50 days. By that time even die-hard fans were thoroughly fed up with baseball's seeming inability to resolve its problems fairly and with dispatch. Talk of a fan boycott never amounted to much, but as players and management look toward their new contract negotiation in 1989—the centenary of the Brotherhood's break with Organized Baseball—both would do well to reflect back on the damage wrought in 1981.

The 1980s have also confronted the game with the drug problem endemic in our society. Baseball's victims are highly publicized and their fall from grace is judged more reprehensible for all the advantages that today's players enjoy—but the game is an American institution reflecting what is wrong with our people as well as what is good in them.

Since Peter Ueberroth's assumption of the commissioner's post prior to the 1985 season, following the 15-year tenure of Bowie Kuhn, baseball has entered the era of high-priced corporate sponsorship, more sophisticated marketing techniques, augmented television revenues and increased overall profitability for the clubs. In the process, baseball has run afoul of its own agreements with players concerning free agency, irritated fans with its acquiescence to the dictates of television regarding postseason play and waffled interminably on the vexed issue of the designated hitter.

Every true baseball fan will have his quibbles with the

present state of things, and will hark back to his personal version of the good old days (yes, the time will come when the 1980s will be seen as the golden decade). But make no mistake about it—baseball is bigger and better than ever and, its inevitable valleys of the future notwithstanding, will only become more so. The game for all America is now played in 79 countries, and is in 1988 (for the first time) an Olympic sport.

The Weather of Our Lives

Ever changing in ways that are so small as to preserve the illusion that "nothing changes in baseball," the game has introduced, in the lifetime of many of you readers: night ball, plane travel, television, integration, bullpen stoppers, expansion, the amateur draft, competitive parity, indoor stadiums, artificial turf, free agency, the designated hitter, aluminum bats and international play. Not far off, perhaps, are further expansion, interleague contests and intercontinental championships.

For fans accustomed to the game's languorous rhythms and conservative resistance to innovation, the changes of the past 20 years in particular seem positively frenetic. Yet for all its changes, baseball has not strayed far from its origins, and in fact has changed far less than other American institutions of equivalent antiquity. What sustains baseball in the hearts of Americans, finally, is not its responsiveness to changes in society nor its propensity for novelty, but its myths, its lore, its records and its essential stability. As Bruce Catton noted in 1959:

A gaffer from the era of William McKinley, abruptly brought back to the second half of the twentieth century, would find very little in modern life that would not seem new, strange and rather bewildering, but put in a good grandstand seat back of first base he would see nothing that was not completely familiar.

It's still a game of bat and ball, played without regard for the clock; a game of 90-foot basepaths, nine innings, nine men in the field; three outs, all out; and three strikes still send you to the bench, no matter whom you know in city hall. It's the national anthem before every game; it's playing catch with your son; it's learning how to win and how to deal with loss, and how to connect with something larger than our selves.

"Baseball," wrote Thomas Wolfe, "has been not merely 'the great national game' but really a part of the whole weather of our lives, of the thing that is our own, of the whole fabric, the million memories of America." Spring comes in America not on the vernal equinox but on opening day; summer sets in with a Memorial Day doubleheader and does not truly end until the last out of the regular season. Winter begins the day after the World Series. Where were you when Bobby Thomson hit the shot heard 'round the world? Or the night Carlton Fisk hit his homer in the 12th? Or when the Mets, with batter after batter one strike away from their loss in the World Series, staged their famous rally? These are milestones in the lives of America and Americans.

We grow up with baseball; we mark—and, for a moment, stop—the passage of time with it; and we grow old with it. It is the game for all America, for all our days.

Is there anything that can evoke spring—the first fine days of April—better than the sound of the ball smacking into the pocket of the big mitt, the sound of the bat as it hits the horsehide . . . ? And is there anything that can tell more about an American summer than, say, the smell of the wooden bleachers in a small-town baseball park, that resinous, sultry, and exciting smell of old dry wood.

—Thomas Wolfe

The Players

It is startling to think how few of the millions who play baseball competitively ever sign a pro contract—one in 40,000—and how few of those hit the big time for even a day (three in a hundred). But statistics have never daunted anyone from pursuing his dream, and for an American boy that dream is to become a star player, leaping above the wall like Kirby Puckett to pull back a home run, or belting a World Series grand slam like Kent Hrbek.

The dream is part hero worship, instructive until a certain age if destructive once beyond. More fundamentally, it is a dream that does not die with the onset of manhood. The dream is to play endlessly, past the time when you are called home for supper, past the time of doing chores, past the time when your body betrays you . . . past time itself. For a child, the grownup world accepts that play is his rightful work, to which he applies a diligence any businessman would envy. For a boy on the cusp of manhood, his salvation is that professional baseball might likewise be termed work in a grownup's world. "When I was a boy growing up in Kansas," an elderly Dwight David Eisenhower recalled, "a friend of mine and I went fishing and as we sat there in the warmth of a summer afternoon on a river bank we talked about what we wanted to do when we grew up. I told him I wanted to be a real major league baseball player, a genuine professional like Honus Wagner. My friend said that he'd like to be President of the United States. Neither of us got our wish."

The bountiful pleasures of baseball begin with the body. There is the indescribable sense of well-being that comes with playing catch, the hearty satisfaction of a line drive whistling from the bat, the joy of running and leaping to the spontaneous choreography of the ball. The elemental acts of baseball—throwing, catching, hitting—are so awesomely complex as to defy words. Is there anything in sport more challenging than hitting a fastball hurled high and tight? More neurologically intricate than judging a fly ball? More sinuously muscular than whipping the ball across the diamond?

While childhood skills are honed by repetition, life's lessons are learned through competition. T-ballers and Little Leaguers, those most rugged individualists, bow to the imperatives of teamwork and perhaps see its virtues. They learn to accept an umpire's verdict, if not endorse it. They learn that honesty is often, if not always, the best policy, that talent unmatched by effort is scorned, and that grace under pressure is so commended because it is so difficult.

Finally, for all of us but a lucky few, the dream of playing big-time baseball is relinquished so we can get on with grownup endeavors. But the dream is never forgotten, only put aside and, in America, never out of reach. Where once the dream connected boys with the world of men, now—perhaps more importantly—it reconnects men with the spirit of boys. Donning a glove for a backyard toss, or watching a ball game, or just reflecting upon our baseball days, we are players again, forever young.

Ball, bat, glove. The basic tools of baseball are for the ages—and the ages of baseball are one: the kid exhibits the "all-business" approach of the pro, who struggles to recall the time when he played just for fun.

Only yesterday the old man was a world-beater of 10 or 12 or 20, with a hop on his fastball and a chip on his shoulder . . . only yesterday. Baseball is intensely felt because it is intensely played, intensely watched, intensely worried over. And when the urgency of youth has faded, the game still is enjoyed intensely because now to the mix of bat and ball and sun and sod are added the unique delights of memory.

Smiles are for the winners, whether they are at the bottom rung of pro ball like the Salt Lake City Trappers of the Summer Class A Pioneer League, who won a professional record 29 consecutive games in 1987, or among the brightest stars in the baseball firmament, like Dwight Gooden and Jesse Orosco of the 1986-champion New York Mets. Yesterday you were down, today you're up. Tomorrow may bring you down again—yes, baseball is more than a little bit like life.

There are those who complain that baseball is too slow, too dull, too old-fashioned. Too much standing around, too much time-wasting. Let's speed it up, they say—make it more like football or basketball or hockey. They see inactivity and they think nothing's going on. How sad! They look but they do not see.

Stretch! You can never tell how far you can go if you don't. The impossible catch sticks in the web; you beat the throw that should have nailed you by 10 feet; you pull a game-winning double down the line off a pitcher whose fastball you never could touch. Three decades after it happened, I can still see myself racing back in center field, my back to home plate, reaching and miraculously foiling destiny's plans for a triple. I can recall everything about those five or six seconds in 1959, but I cannot explain how I came to make that catch, unless it was simply that I stretched farther than I knew I could.

(Pages 42-43)
How does a man from Alabama, by way of New York, win the hearts of San Francisco? The singularity of Willie Mays is not the answer; any player who wears a city's baseball uniform becomes a hometown hero, no matter how he got there. These men are professionals whose services are up for bid and whose bags often are packed—and yet we call them our own, take personal, even civic pride in their accomplishments. Strange thing, fandom. Strange and wonderful.

THE GAME FOR ALL AMERICA

You can't play the game without the baseball, and there's the rub. To a toddler, a soft rubber ball is a friendly object, an inviting toy. When a youngster first encounters a baseball, however, and receives his baptismal bruise, he learns that this particular ball may be his enemy and he had better stay out of its path. But that's no way to become a player—a player has to overcome fear and stand up to the ball. It's easier said than done, though, and that's why softballers routinely bat .600 while major leaguers aspire to hit half that.

As Hamlet is greater than any actor who ever played the part, so too is baseball greater than its greatest players. Today's stars, like Dave Parker, should savor their time in the sun, for their successors are on the playgrounds by the millions, hard at work.

Of play and players, what is remembered after all? The exhilaration of teamwork or the individual triumph? In the great American game as in the very concept of the republic, the two are indivisible.

Boy meets bat, bat meets ball, the romance begins. As they say about learning to ride a bicycle, once you learn how, you never forget, no matter how long it's been since your last ride. Still, even the most experienced rider, or player, will need to get back to basics if he is to keep his skills sharp. Baseball is a game of renewal, of beginning and beginning again, with each season, game and at-bat. So tee it up and line it out!

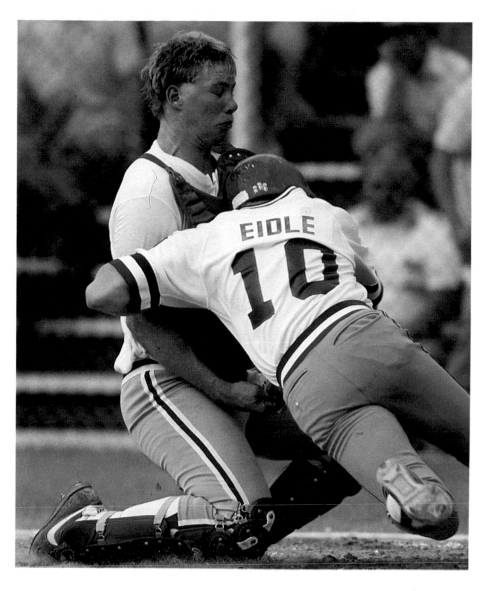

No pain, no gain. Baseball the beautiful also can be baseball the brutal, but that, too, is part of the game's appeal. Alexander Cartwright and his Knickerbockers of the 1840s, when they formulated the first rules, never envisioned such unseemly behavior as barreling into the catcher or plunking a batter in the ribs. But earlier versions of baseball than Cartwright's were less refined, less beholden to the genteel ways of cricket, and the fusing of their rough spirit with the new rules transformed a gentleman's field exercise to a nation's pastime.

An afternoon at the ball park affords a continual coupling of opposites: the cool contemplation of the bullpen with the fervent exchange of ideas at home plate; the stealthy purpose of the pitcher with the forthright, though sometimes feeble, response of the batter.

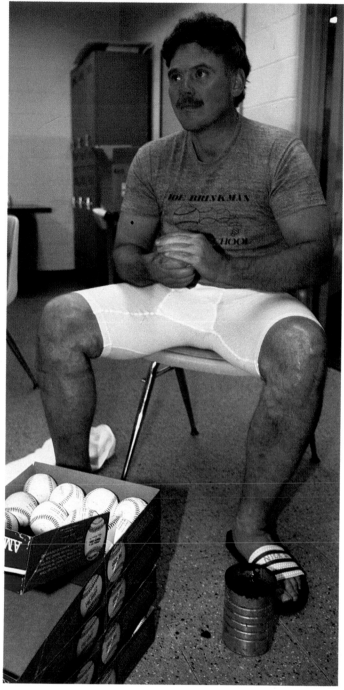

Base bandit, eh? As Arthur (Bugs) Baer said of Ping Bodie, another improbably constituted brigand of the basepaths, "He had larceny in his heart, but his feet were honest." So too are the yawns and mud-rubbing drudgery that can be found anywhere, be it a Little League park or Municipal Stadium, home of the Reading Phillies.

Pop quiz: What do the photograph and baseball have in common? Answer: They both officially were invented in 1839—though baseball's debut is in fact tougher to pin down—and both stop time, permitting us to retain in our mind's eye what in "real life" passes before us too quickly.

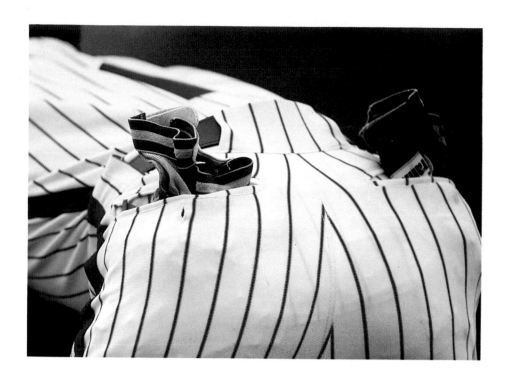

Baseball can be cruel, and kids can learn valuable lessons through the countless small frustrations of an ordinary game: the full-count call that went the other way; the split-second stumble in the batter's box that turned a hit into just another close play at first; the blistering drive caught in deepest center field. But where character is truly forged is in the crucible of crushing failure. If self-knowledge and resilience emerge from the ordeal, then another lesson is taught: that in today's defeat are planted the seeds of tomorrow's victory.

THE GAME FOR ALL AMERICA

He was out by a mile! No, safe by an eyelash! When you've made baseball your life, as Gene Mauch has, you've seen it all a thousand times over—and yet every day you see something out on that field that you've never seen before. That's baseball—endlessly repeated rhythms, ever-changing detail.

The game for all America, yes, but maybe more: For the first time, baseball, with its budding Mark McGwires, Cory Snyders and Will Clarks, is an official competition in the 1988 Olympics; Far East teams have dominated recent Little League World Series; baseball diplomacy bodes to promote harmony with our estranged neighbors, Cuba and Nicaragua. It is now 100 years since Albert Spalding set off on a round-the-world tour, accompanied by two major league squads, to spread the gospel of baseball. Perhaps the nations are now ready for his vision of one world, united by baseball.

Roy Campanella said it best: "You have to be a man to be a big leaguer, but you have to have a lot of little boy in you, too." We look back with particular fondness on our baseball heroes who radiated that puckishness of youth—Rube Waddell, Rabbit Maranville, Lefty Gomez, Satchel Paige and, more recently, Mark Fidrych and Bill Lee.

High fives. And eights. And elevens. If you were ever lucky enough to be part of a winning team, at any level of play, you remember exactly how ecstatic these guys feel. Winners have to be lucky, sure, to have this kind of fun, but they didn't get to be winners just by being lucky or by having fun. Luck is the residue of design, and victory the fruit of endurance.

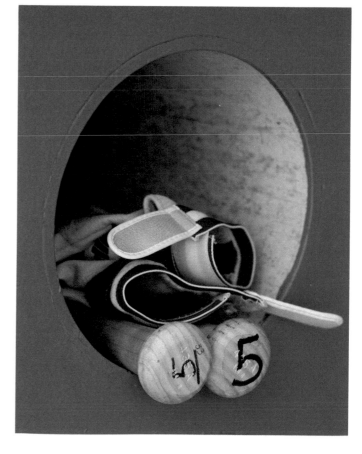

Players have often enough encountered trouble with their eyesight, or an umpire's. Although veteran arbiter Bill Klem retired in 1940 because he could only see with one eye, four years later, Branch Rickey demanded his services for some spring exhibition games. "I got by fine," Klem said. "I wasn't surprised because I never thought eyesight was the most important thing in umpiring. The most important things are guts, honesty, common sense, a desire for fair play and an understanding of human nature."

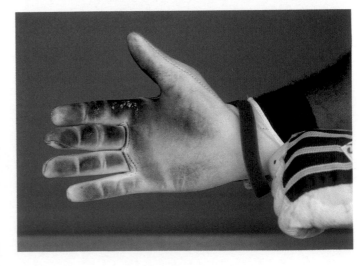

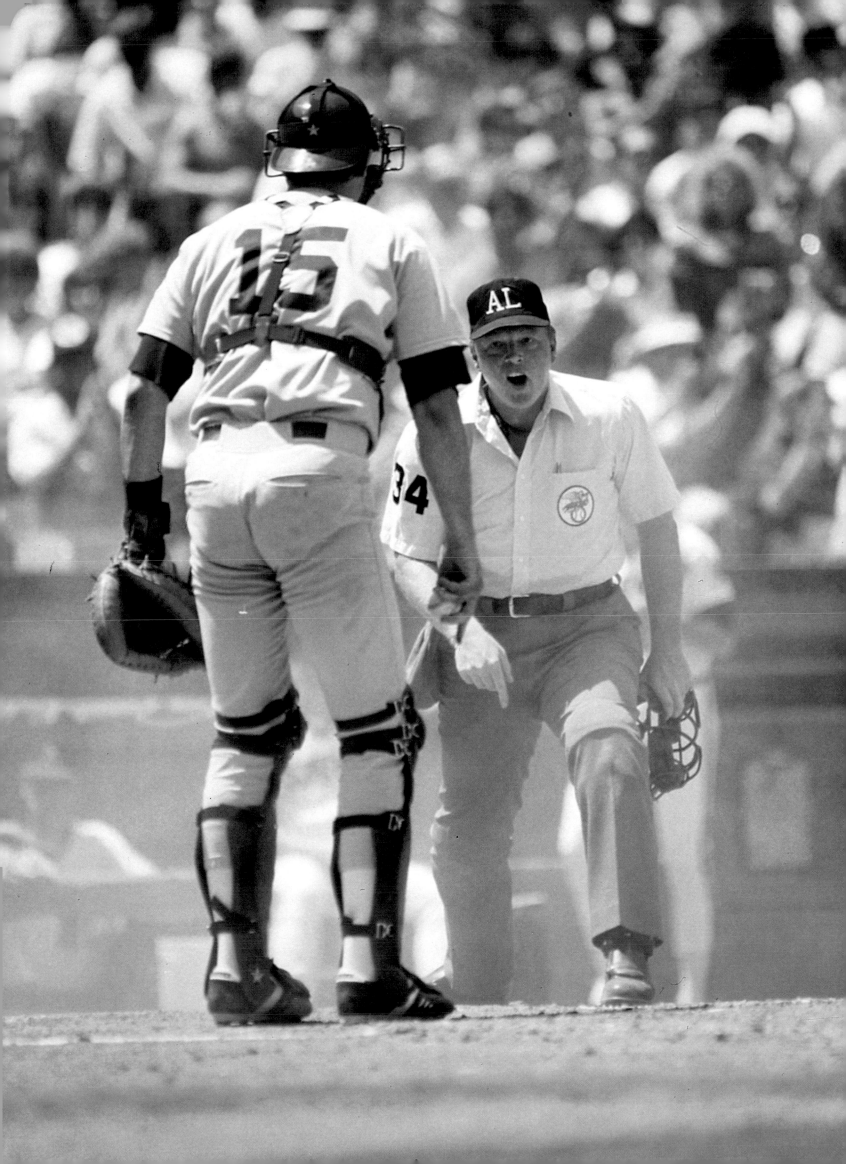

American League President Bobby Brown, once a hard-hitting third baseman for the New York Yankees, has said: "The art of hitting is the art of getting your pitch to hit." This may not be as memorable as Wee Willie Keeler's maxim, "Keep your eye on the ball and hit 'em where they ain't," but it surely is a superior piece of advice.

From the dewy clarity of a spring morning's workout, through the shimmering heat of a midsummer brushback, on up to the cold fire of baseball's autumnal climax, this is a game for all seasons. At the end of October, when a young Minnesotan's thoughts have traditionally turned iceward, baseball roared in the Hubert H. Humphrey Metrodome. Suddenly, unimaginably, players, twin cities and state alike went baseball mad. The Twins' stunning World Series victory would keep the North Country warm all winter, fanning the flames of the hot stove league until spring came round again.

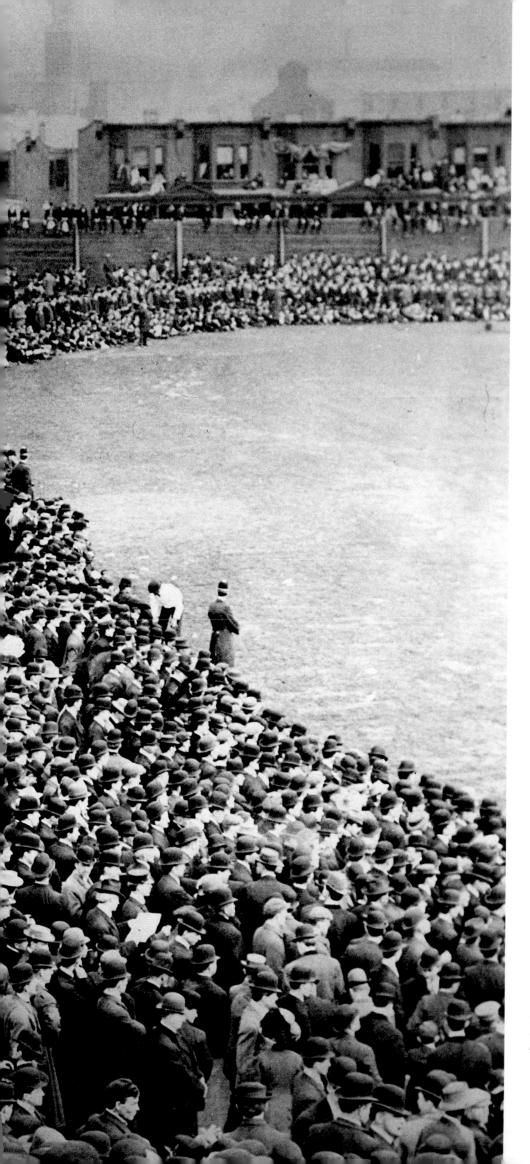

The
Fans

Baseball binds America. Its rhythms and rituals resonate across the great divides of generation, politics, religion and economics to connect our people as nothing else can. To a nation whose proverbial melting pot is all too often a bubbling caldron of incompatibility, baseball offers its model of bleacher democracy, a true community of like minds and spirits and language that enables a son to educate his father about the leadoff man's poor on-base average, or a janitor to confide to a bank president his low regard for the visiting team's bullpen.

At a ball game, as in a place of worship, no one is alone in the crowd. As Robert Coover wrote, "I felt like I was part of something there, you know, like in church, except it was more real than any church, and I joined in the scorekeeping, hollering, the eating of hot dogs and drinking of Cokes and beer, and for a while I even had the idea that ball stadiums, and not European churches, were the real American holy places."

But America's devotion to baseball is not fully explained by our craving for a sense of unity and connection with other Americans. We are fans because the game also appeals to our local pride, our pleasure in thinking of ourselves as, yes, Americans, but nonetheless different from residents of other towns, other states, other regions. This illuminates not only fans' interest in Little League and American Legion ball, but even in minor and major league teams.

Just reflect on how jaded New York glowed with pride when the Mets won their championships; or how delighted Oaklanders were in the 1970s to thumb their noses at those stuck-up neighbors across the bay; or how the economically troubled cities of Detroit and Pittsburgh took heart as their teams tasted success.

Finally, we are fans because we never really stopped being players and, in the words of Bruce Catton, baseball "celebrates the vicarious triumph. The spectator can identify himself completely with the player, and the epochal feat becomes, somehow, an achievement of his own. Babe Ruth, mocking the Chicago Cubs, pointing to the distant bleachers and then calmly hitting the ball into those bleachers, took a host of Walter Mittys with him when he jogged around the bases."

The game moves along slowly, seamlessly, from inning to inning, game to game, season to season. The players and crowd and script change, yet stay the same. Our lives move along, too, yet in our images of ourselves, we stay the same. Just sit in the grandstand and listen to the patter: Why didn't the right fielder dive for that looper? (We would have at least given the effort.) How could that bum of a batter fail to make contact with the tying run on third and one out? (We would have shortened up our swing.) Why didn't the pitcher work around the cleanup hitter rather than challenge him? (We would have been more clever.)

Our bottoms are perched in the stands, yes, or on the couch before the TV, but our hearts are on the field.

It is late in the game and the home team trails by five runs. The true fan's response may be contemplative or stalwart, but never despairing. One of the first lessons he or she learns is that in baseball anything, absolutely anything, can happen.

Inside every rotund, superannuated, implausibly decked-out rooter is a trim youth of 16, potential unlimited and limits unposted. That potential is out from under wraps at the ball park, where people are different—less reserved, more approachable, more *themselves*. What is the magic that the game works on us? Is it a transference of powers from player to fan, visible in the passing of an autograph, invisible in its lightening of the spirit? Our heroes are larger than life, and their accomplishments inflate us as well, making us special for a moment.

Victory is so sweet that it would be miserly to confine its joys to the players. That's where the fans come in. They may be fickle in their affections for a player, but they are constant in their affections for their team, determinedly riding the roller coaster of victory and defeat, glorying in the moments at the summit and suffering stoically through the sloughs of despond. Ask a Giants fan—those deep valleys make the trip to the top all the more gratifying.

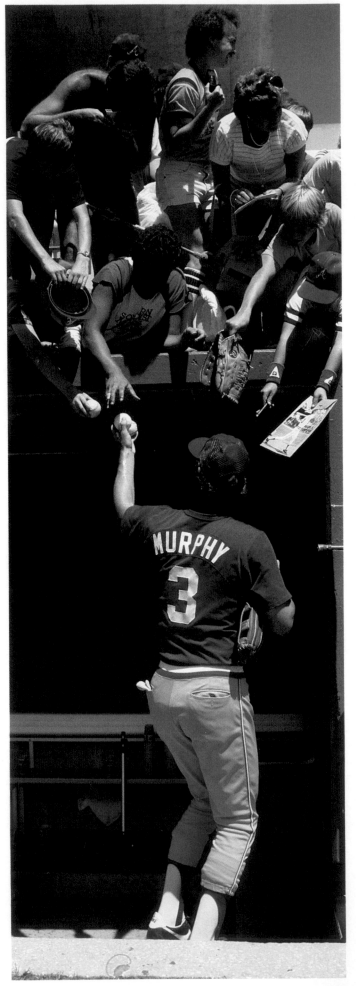

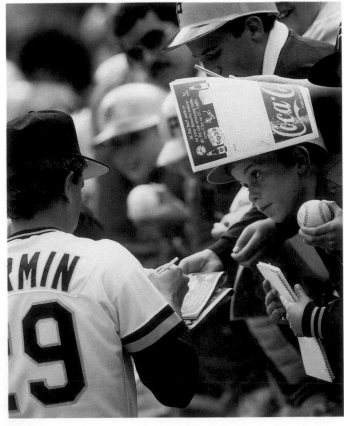

THE GAME FOR ALL AMERICA

The competition for autographs at the ball park is fierce, and to be successful kids must learn how to be persistent while remaining polite. It's an art that pays off with such superstars as Reggie Jackson and Dale Murphy, whose reserves of patience and energy are tested daily but not tapped out; if the younger players are sometimes surly, it may be that they have not yet learned what Jackson and Murphy recognized long ago: that without the ordinary fan, there are no stars.

Remember what it was like to be in a ball park when you were, say, 8 years old? How incredibly huge the field was? How vivid the expanse of green? How the speckled colors of the crowd danced in the sun? Maybe you lingered after the game for one final hotdog and an Orange Crush and a thrilling, if disorienting, glimpse of a demigod in street clothes.

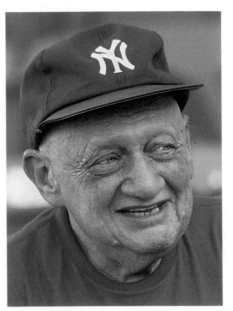

THE GAME FOR ALL AMERICA

Like the plaid of the clan or the mystic rites of the lodge, wearing the team cap is a badge of your allegiance. "LET'S foil 'em"—the fan is no mere spectator but a participant, and the fervor of his rooting will have a bearing on the outcome. In the drama that is a baseball game, he is a true player.

"Baseball is the working man's game," Bill Veeck once said. "A baseball crowd is a beer-drinking crowd, not a mixed-drink crowd." In the same vein, W.R. Burnett wrote, "The true fan is not only violently partisan, but very noisy. . . . I used to amuse myself with wondering what would happen if a group of fans of this order would turn up at a tennis match or a golf meet."

It's about the ball, this game we love. It's about the bat and the glove, too, but mostly, it's about the ball. To have the world in the palm of your hand—we get a glimmer of what that feels like whenever we grasp that little globe. "Play ball!"—an anthem for the generations.

THE GAME FOR ALL AMERICA

The smiles of a summer afternoon at the ball field.
Wrestling with a hot dog or acting like one. Feeling
the chain link of father and son at an adorable game
in Detroit or at the scene of triumphs past and trials
future.

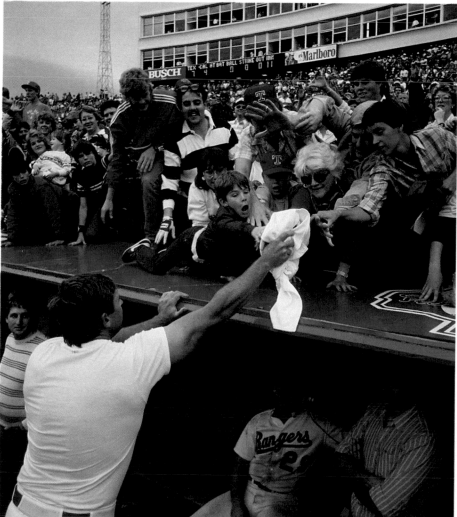

For Philip Roth, "baseball was a kind of secular church that reached into every class and region of the nation and bound millions upon millions of us together in common concerns, loyalties, rituals, enthusiasms and antagonisms." Here, celebrants of baseball line up before their pews, the Rangers' Larry Parrish doffs his vestment, a nun extends her parish to Dodger Stadium and a grizzled disciple glories in the game.

Autograph mania. Society will frown upon these big-game hunters' capture of Gary Carter and the mounting of his head above the mantel, so they content themselves with paper trophies, which they mount in scrapbooks or, dismayingly often, sell.

Between the throwing out of the first ball and the final exultation of victory a fan can go through a lifetime's range of emotions.

Fanhood is the communal sharing of individual accomplishment and failing. The extended family of baseball is there to comfort, to instruct, to encourage, to celebrate. And like your own family, it is there to convey tradition and ensure continuity. The measure of a fan may be figured by the number of Little League World Series pins on his cap.

That baseball is a game of fathers and sons is a commonplace wisdom; less commonly observed is the notion that baseball also links generations of mothers and sons, and fathers and daughters. Doris Kearns Goodwin wrote, "If I close my eyes against the sun, all at once I am back at Ebbets Field, a young girl once more in the presence of my father, watching the players of my youth on the grassy field below. There is magic in this moment, for when I open my eyes and see my sons in the place where my father once sat, I feel an invisible bond between our three generations, an anchor of loyalty linking my sons to the grandfather whose face they never saw. . . ."

A cowbell: Hilda Chester's legacy from the Brooklyn Dodgers' Symphoney Band of the 1930s to the San Antonio Dodgers' Booster Club of today. The ball park is a place to have a good time in a raucous sort of way—without fear that a Phillie Phanatic's antics will spoil the phun for a Perrier-sipping sort in the next seat. Yet it is also a place for peaceable pleasures—obtaining a hero's token or just pretending to be him.

THE GAME FOR ALL AMERICA

Baseball is the game for all America and all Americans, boys and men, girls and women. It is a game of red, white and blue, and a game of black and white and yellow and brown and all shades in between.

Day is done. The sun recedes and the damp rises. The dogs and the nuts and the suds sit heavy in the stomach; though it is time to go, the mind and body say, "Stay." After the game is over, after the day is through, it's hard to pick up and head home.

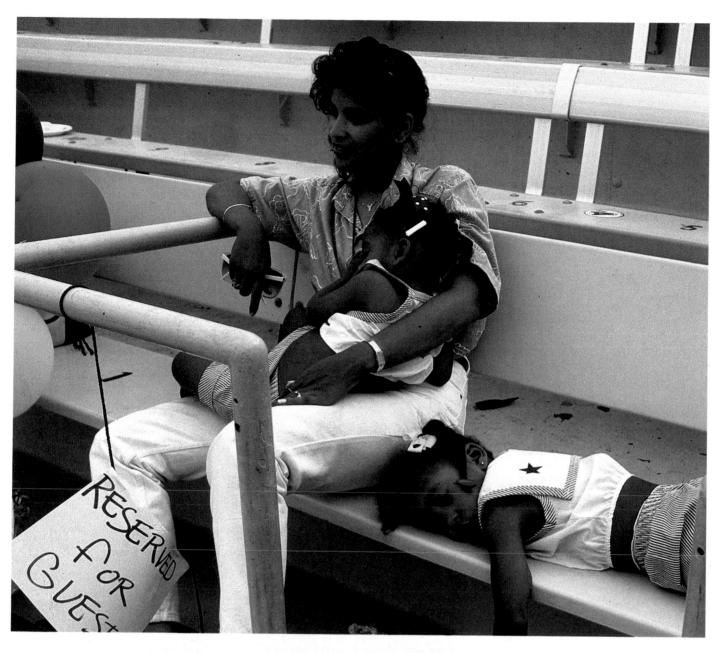

Everybody needs a hero, someone to look up to and try one day to match. The young admirer of the Chicago White Sox perhaps imagines himself one day the equal of Harold Baines; the Cubs' Ryne Sandberg offers himself for the photographic fantasies of Cub fans; and in a neat reversal at the Little League World Series, Number 16's dad, long his son's hero, becomes his fan.

THE GAME FOR ALL AMERICA

What thrills and laughter this glorious game brings us! What memories! From watching our sons grow up in baseball to marveling at our hometown team's defiance of the laws of probability, we are a fortunate people to have baseball as our national game. Surely if it were to be gone from our lives, something would come along to take its place. But you'll never convince me that whatever came along would be any better, or even nearly as good.

The Workers

Ever since July 21, 1858, when an admission fee was first charged for watching a baseball game, our national pastime has been both a sport and a business. "Too much of a sport to be called a business," Cubs Owner Phil Wrigley once said, "and too much of a business to be called a sport." But unlike General Motors or IBM, baseball in America is everyone's business.

At every field across our land, from sandlot to stadium, the double paradox is the same: Some must work so others can play, and others must play so some can work. There are workers like the groundkeepers, whose labors affect the play; and there are workers like the scorecard vendors, whose livelihood stands apart from the play but derives totally from it.

Entrepreneurs and employees, functionaries and hustlers—baseball embraces them all. They have chosen to work in baseball not because it holds out the promise of vast riches, but because their toil allows them to be part of the game. The sense of vicarious and communal celebration that binds a nation of fans likewise bonds baseball's workers with its players.

Could a hawker of peanuts and pennants as easily sell ice cream from a truck or refrigerators at Sears? Sure, and more profitably, too. But peanuts and pennants get him into the park. For a dealer in baseball cards and other memorabilia, the story is the same, but his "park" is the larger one that National League President A. Bartlett Giamatti has termed "the green fields of the mind."

Baseball requires no oath of loyalty or love from its workers. You can see how they feel about the game—the ticket takers and basepath sweepers and soda sellers—by looking at the spring in their step and the beam on their faces. These folks are past being players, and more than fans; if life is, as Freud said, love and work, they have made baseball their life.

The baseball life can mean moving from player to manager to front office, like a Connie Mack or Clark Griffith, or more recently a Bobby Cox or Lou Piniella. But the baseball life is also moving from Little League player to booster to scoreboard operator to banquet organizer. The baseball life is a life of play, joyously masquerading as work.

Shooting fish in a barrel, that's the way you might think of selling baseball trinkets at a baseball park. But it's not that easy, or this bountifully laden vendor wouldn't be working the sparse crowd so energetically. In contrast, the usher's uniform lends him a lordly air of repose as he surveys his domain. This is *his* field. Players come and players go. He remains.

THE GAME FOR ALL AMERICA

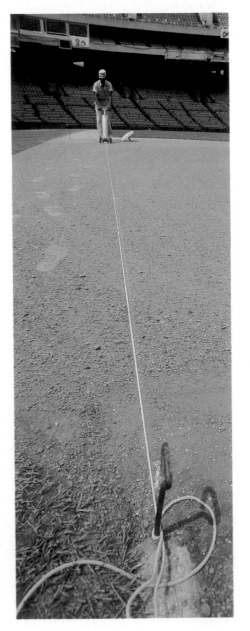

THE GAME FOR ALL AMERICA

The groundkeeper, like Kansas City's George Toma, has a sense of his importance in baseball's scheme of things. After all, he gets to keep the ground; the players only get to use it. Whether chalking the baselines in Baltimore, protecting the American Legion World Series field from the ravages of the elements or nurturing every blade of grass—the groundcrew's efforts are best when unnoticed in the course of the game.

There's nothing glamorous about working at the ball park. Here, men are at work, absorbed in their tasks: Fernando Valenzuela's agent puts the radar gun to his client's screwball; trash sweepers ready the Williamsport, Pa., stadium for the next day's round of the Little League World Series; a solitary seat cleaner is undaunted by the magnitude of his mission at the Maine Guides' park in Old Orchard Beach.

THE GAME FOR ALL AMERICA

Our sublime day of baseball in the sun begins in the stadium's subterranean depths where the clubhouse manager presides. Fans seldom give him a thought, but look to the split of the World Series purse for how the players regard him. The ball girl is that rare thing in baseball, an innovation that most people like. They're cute, they occasionally corral a foul grounder and they're less controversial than the designated hitter. A ticket seller before a big ball game is like St. Peter standing at the portals of paradise, holding in his or her hands the word on an applicant's fate. There *is* one pair of seats behind home plate? Heaven lies just past the turnstiles.

THE GAME FOR ALL AMERICA

THE GAME FOR ALL AMERICA

THE GAME FOR ALL AMERICA

(Pages 126-127)
The down-to-earth artist of the Texas Rangers paints the team logo in satisfied solitude, knowing that in a matter of hours his art will be appreciated by an audience larger than most painters ever achieve in a lifetime.

THE GAME FOR ALL AMERICA

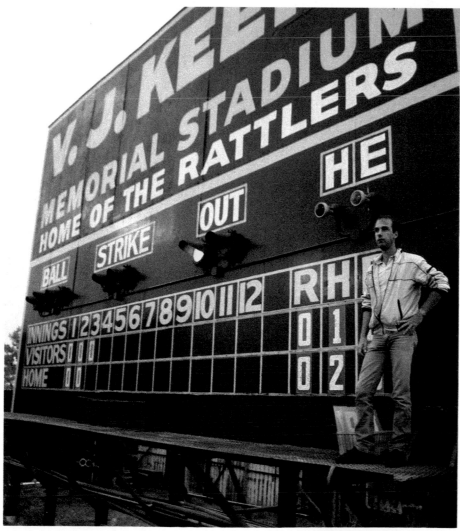

Grass! Cut it, drag it, sweep it, drain it. Pamper it. Revel in the smell, the look, the feel of it. Baseball's antecedents, primitive games of bat and ball played in England and Germany in the medieval period, in Mayan Mexico and the Egypt of the pharaohs, were truly rites of spring, fertility ceremonies for mankind and the earth itself. It is harder today to sense the stirrings of spring in a carpet of ersatz grass, but if your imagination is strong you don't even have to close your eyes to catch the thrill of the real thing.

They also serve who only sweep and rake. The game may last two and a half hours, but game day begins early and ends late, and enlists the aid of legions of workers. The baseballs get a mud bath in Baltimore and the foul lines get a dusting of lime at the American Legion World Series. In Milwaukee's County Stadium, a Brewers' broomer spruces up and the groundcrew lovingly levels the batter's box (so that the leadoff batter can promptly dig a hole for his back foot).

THE GAME FOR ALL AMERICA

Baseball has offered friendly turf for concessionaires from its earliest days. Mongers of fruits, nuts, soda and lemonade competed with peddlers of beer and hard liquor from the 1860s on. As tastes changed in the 1880s, the fare expanded to include coconut pies, sandwiches, pickled eggs and (ugh) tripe. Hot dogs—or "red hots," as the reddish dachshund-shaped sausages were called—made their ball park debut at some point in the century's first decade. And today there are nachos and pretzels and ice cream and bratwurst and you name it. And amazingly, it all tastes better at the ball park.

At the beginning of major league competiton in 1876, players bought, laundered and transported their own uniforms, and the whole team's bats could be contained in a single canvas bag. The players tended the grounds before the game and, if out injured or not in the starting lineup, worked the turnstiles or the ticket booth. Are today's stars, long accustomed to conducting their profession on a pedestal, aware that they stand on a vast base of supporting players?

Thomas Boswell wrote, "All baseball fans can be divided into two groups: those who come to batting practice and the others. Only those in the first category have much chance of amounting to anything. . . ." There are fans whose aristocracy exceeds even that of the batting-practice buffs: the ones who get a kick out of seeing a park prettied up for the ball.

If music be the food of glove, play on. Nancy Faust is the organist at Chicago's Comiskey Park, the major leagues' oldest stadium, where the fans have adored their White Sox since 1910 (only two years after the composition of "Take Me Out to the Ball Game"). At Wrigley Field—built in 1914 as Weeghman Park, home of the Chicago Whales of the rival Federal League—workers have had to tend not only the grass but also, since 1937, the ivy on the outfield walls. And it was in this park in 1914 that baseball marked one of its myriad little-known firsts: the establishment of the first permanent ball park concession stand. (Previously, all collectibles and comestibles were sold by strolling vendors or ball park restaurants.) Today, offering everything from tamales to team-logo T-shirts, the concession stand is a standard fixture of every park.

THE GAME FOR ALL AMERICA

Remember the first time your father took you to a major league game? It's amazing how few of the on-field events stick in the memory, but, oh, the hot dogs and the scorecard and, most prized, the souvenir—these linger glowingly into adulthood, as they will for your children.

THE GAME FOR ALL AMERICA

Ball park workers seldom get to tip their caps to the crowd, seldom get to hear the cheers. They toil in obscurity, their efforts most worthy of note when least noted. You have to admire the spirit that drives a man to set his base precisely in the corner of Alexander Cartwright's square when no one else will know if it's one or two degrees off. Baseball's workers are a dedicated bunch.

THE GAME FOR ALL AMERICA

Those big pretzels with mustard are big in Philly. Hot dogs are hot stuff in Cincinnati, commonly known as Porkopolis a century ago. Popcorn is popular at ball parks in the heartland, where peanuts for some reason do poorly. And beer has been an integral part of baseball for a century—indeed, it was the National League's refusal to permit the sale of beer to the sunbroiled patrons of Cincinnati that gave rise to a whole major league, the "beer-and-whiskey circuit" American Association of the 1880s. One of life's joys is the combination of a cold brew, a hot dog and a day game.

Baseball is entertainment, and within the chest of many a vendor beats the heart of an entertainer. Some peanut men hand the bag to the patron seated at the aisle, expecting him to pass it along to you. Others, like the dexterous slinger at Dodger Stadium, elevate peanut vending to the realm of art. How does he do it? Why isn't he down on the field with the other players? I remember when I was a boy a peanut man at the Polo Grounds lobbing a bag right to me over eight aisles of fans intent on the ball game, then hollering to me to toss him my quarter. Easy for him to say (and do)! I was terrified I'd make an errant toss and waited for him to wend his way up to my row.

THE GAME FOR ALL AMERICA

Despite the domed stadiums and computerized scoreboard displays, we cherish baseball because it remains a proud anachronism, reminding us in a thousand small details of the idyllic past that forms the core of our national mythology. Pulling together—teamwork—united America's agrarian society in a way that today's industrial or corporate efforts do not. Battening down in the face of a storm, haying on a hot summer day, spinning out cotton candy at the county fair—the bygone joys of community are relived in the customs of the ball field.

THE GAME FOR ALL AMERICA

The workers know that morning, before the players and fans start drifting in, is the ball park's glory. Walking onto that vast expanse of green circled by rows of empty seats fills you with awe and wonder, like standing alone in a great cathedral. The call of the earth and grass and air is irresistible—work the land, make it grow and prosper.

THE GAME FOR ALL AMERICA

Who said players have a monopoly on fun? In the majors, at least, now that megabucked baseball players turn to the stock market indices in the newspaper before checking their own stats, the workers may share more of a sense of play than the players.

The Field

Why did Cubs management, some 50 years ago, plant vines on the brick walls of Wrigley Field? So the fans coming to see their Bearcubs cavort in God's sunlight would feel as if they were enjoying a picnic on the green, or a nostalgic trip back to America's preindustrial Eden. After all, Wrigley was not a magnificent "stadium" or "coliseum" or "dome," but simply a *field,* a field of play, like Forbes and Crosley and Ebbets and Braves and, in baseball's very beginning, the Elysian Fields of Hoboken, N. J.

It's interesting that until 1923, when the Yankees opened "the house that Ruth built" in the wilds of the Bronx, baseball had no stadium (Washington's site, opened in 1911 as National Park, only later came to be known as Griffith Stadium, as Detroit's Navin Field went on to become Briggs Stadium). Before that, the places where professionals assembled to play went by the plain old names that today are applied to amateur lots in America's hamlets and towns—park, grounds and field.

Here's a telling bit of trivia: In 1922, major league baseball had no stadiums among its 14 sites (the Yankees and Giants shared New York's Polo Grounds, the Browns and Cards shared St. Louis' Sportsman's Park); there was one bowl (Baker), one grounds (Polo) and the rest were equally divided between fields and parks. Of today's 26 big league sites, 18 are stadiums, three are domes, one is a coliseum. Three are parks, one is a field.

That says a lot about how America has changed, even in its perspective on baseball. And yet, of all American institutions, baseball has changed least. And therein lies the strength of its hold on our hearts. To a kid, a day out at the ball park is still the stuff of dreams, even if the ball park is a stadium or the day is a night or the out is indoors. At a dusty Little League park where the grass is mangy and the pebbles fly up with every step, or a domed stadium where the players can look more like computer graphics than human beings, baseball remains baseball.

Players need a place to play, and the ball parks in their different configurations become, in a way, players themselves. Baseball, demanding only a diamond of uniform size, offers so much latitude for shaping the action—outfield distances, wall heights, turf style, foul area, elevation, prevailing wind, and more. Only golf imposes fewer restrictions on the field of play than baseball. Football, basketball, soccer, hockey—these games are played pretty much the same at every site, even though there are pronounced home-field advantages. But does anything in those sports parallel the Yankees' bypassing of Whitey Ford when his turn in the rotation came up in Boston? Or Andre Dawson's offer to sign a blank contract if he could play half his games in Wrigley Field?

In fact, baseball's oldest and quirkiest parks—heirlooms like Fenway and Wrigley and Comiskey and Tiger Stadium—become not mere players but stars, as Ebbets and Forbes and the Polo Grounds were in their day, affecting the way the game was played more than any player. After the wave of cookie-cutter stadiums in the 1960s and 1970s (Richie Hebner once said, "I stand at the plate in Philadelphia and I honestly don't know whether I'm in Pittsburgh, Cincinnati, St. Louis or Philly"), it's refreshing to see newer baseball parks—in Toronto and Minneapolis—displaying some of the wonderfully weird traits that once seemed gone forever.

Nature's grandeur is made grander by a bit of man's taming influence. Here the jewel in the crown is the California Angels' spring training field; the setting, Palm Springs.

It's a matter of scale, of course, but from sandlot to stadium, baseball links us. The game is the same and the feelings are the same—from the Little League World Series in Williamsport (facing page, top) to the Khoury League tri-state finals in St. Louis (left), from the Big League World Series in Fort Lauderdale (above) to baseball's version of the Big Top, Houston's Astrodome.

Bright lights, big city. The Dodgers fled Brooklyn for several reasons, particularly the small seating capacity of Ebbets Field, the lack of parking space in densely populated Flatbush and the lure of lucre in Los Angeles, then the major American city without a major league team. And after a four-year stay in the Coliseum, a football stadium that yielded only 251 feet to left field, the Dodgers settled into their beautiful new home at Chavez Ravine. Annual attendance exceeding 3 million has become commonplace and Dodger Stadium—now, strangely, one of baseball's oldest parks—has become a classic.

As little folks in a big place, we stand in awe of the concrete-and-steel stadiums with their massive scale. Remember how dark and cool and secret it felt to prowl the caverns under the grandstand, and how dazzling was that first view of the great green field when we emerged from the tunnel? Yet as grownups, many of us come to savor, even prefer, the air of small-time baseball. And in all of baseball anywhere, is there anything more forlorn than these words: "Game Called, Rain"?

THE GAME FOR ALL AMERICA

For aficionados of ball park architecture, the best of the new is Kansas City's Royals Stadium. Its unique waterfalls and fountains run for 322 feet along an embankment in right center, and the light show makes every night at the ball park the Fourth of July, which is baseball as it ought to be. Kansas City's former tenants, the Athletics, moved to Oakland in 1968. There the Coliseum (below) came to be called the Mausoleum as the franchise hit hard times in the 1970s, but new management has spruced it up and created a new baseball atmosphere. In 1966 Busch Stadium (right), with the Arch forming a sort of halo, replaced Sportsman's Park in St. Louis, thus ending exactly a century of baseball played at the intersection of Spring and Sullivan and Grand and Dodier.

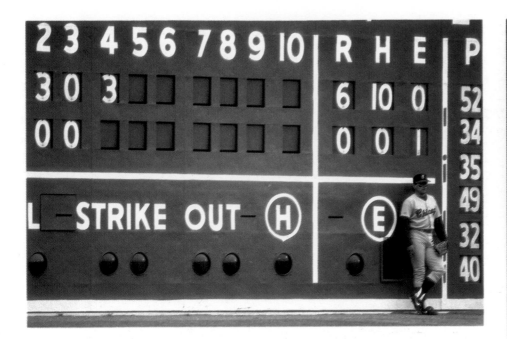

Baseball presents a living heritage, a game poised between the powerful undertow of seasons past and the hope of next day, next week, next year. Past and present come together satisfyingly at the grand old game's grand old fields, with their antique scoreboards and their shapes defined by neighborhoods, not parking lots. Here, Fenway Park, Wrigley Field and, to the right, Municipal Stadium in Reading, Pa.

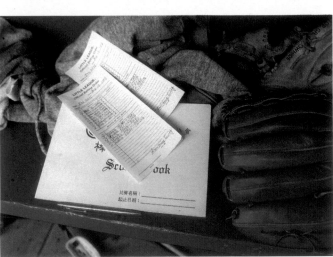

Light and shadow, man-made and God-given. Baseball under artificial light was first tried out at Nantasket Beach, Mass., in 1880, but not at the major league level until 55 years later. First seen by many as sacrilege—on the order of, say, the designated hitter or the aluminum bat—night baseball is now more common than the day variety. In 1960, Chicago White Sox Owner Bill Veeck gave baseball another dubious innovation, the exploding scoreboard; it was replaced at Comiskey Park in 1982 by the now ubiquitous Diamond Vision, or double vision. In the space of a generation, baseball has gone from instant replay on the home screen to simultaneous replay at the park. Future replay cannot be far off.

(Pages 170-171)
An evening under the arcs is not as lazily satisfying as a day in the sun but it is more . . . electric. Here is a thrilling panorama of a night game at The Big A, as Anaheim Stadium was called when it was opened in 1966. In 1981, when the outfield was enclosed and a double deck added, some called it The Bigger A.

THE GAME FOR ALL AMERICA

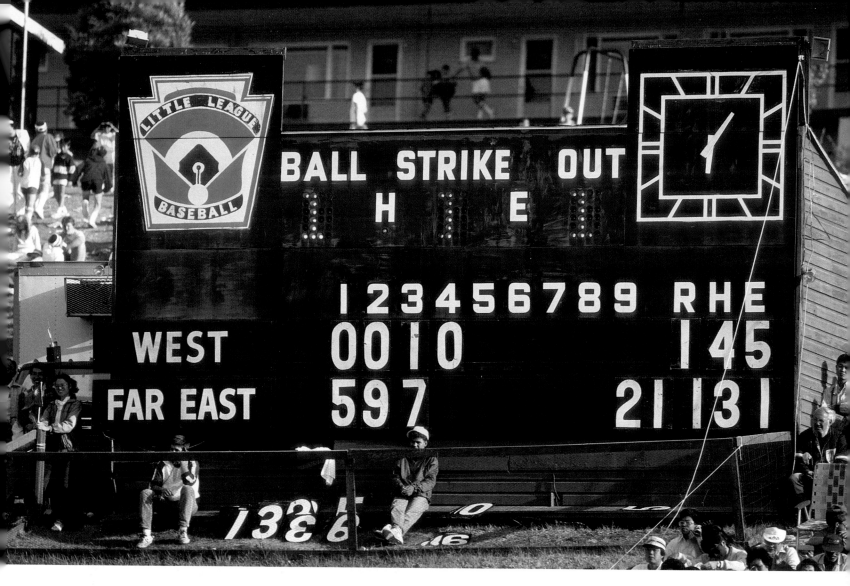

If the Battle of Waterloo was won, as Lord Nelson declared, on the playing fields of Eton, then there is a worrisome implication to be drawn from recent contests at Williamsport, Pa., home of the Little League World Series. But if East is East and West is West, at least the twain meet on the baseball field. On the facing page at the top is a model of perfect harmony: the brick and the ivy of Wrigley Field. Below that is the home of the Reading Phillies of the Eastern League, and alongside is the entrance to the most perfectly named of all ball parks: the home of the Maine Guides in Orchard Beach, Me., known simply and officially as "The Ballpark."

When our civilization lies in ruins millennia from now, like ancient Egypt or the Peru of the Incas, what will tomorrow's archaeologists make of these structures? Will they see in the remains of Riverfront Stadium a temple for the observance of seasonal rites? Will they interpret the baselines and markings of the College World Series at Omaha as landing strips for extraterrestrials? Will they theorize that the Metrodome was a giant burial mound? Make no mistake about it—these stadiums and ball parks are American landmarks, just as the ball courts at Chichen Itza in the Yucatan reveal the mysteries of Mayan culture.

THE GAME FOR ALL AMERICA

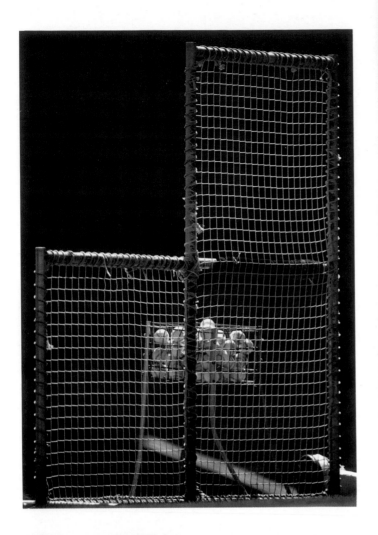

Cage within a cage, grid within a grid, game within a game. World within a world—that is baseball, a mirror to our lives. And the ball park is a special place where all of life's struggles are played out in small.

THE GAME FOR ALL AMERICA

The long view—perspective—is what you miss watching the game on television. That's why real fans continue to say, as often as they can, "Take Me Out to the Ball Game." Real fans will not content themselves solely with a television director's idea of what they should be seeing. There have been dire predictions in recent years that first pay television and then cable would reduce baseball to a television-studio event, with no need for a live audience. And yet, with ever more baseball available on the tube, the numbers attending the games continue to rise. At the park (or from the rooftop overlooking the park, as on Waveland Avenue behind Wrigley Field) there's so much to take in besides the action.

There is an undeniable beauty in the image of a simple ball field at sundown or a majestically situated ball park in the glare of the afternoon (the former, Stevens Point, Wis.; the latter, Derks Field in Salt Lake City). No one would describe Flushing's Shea Stadium, home of the Mets, as beautiful. Nonetheless, it has an undeniable architectural presence, and more important, it is the storehouse of millions of memories. That is, ultimately, what makes all ball parks beautiful.

It begins in the brightness of spring, as a weary Indian trudges back to the clubhouse after a hard day's training. It skyrockets in the heat of summer, when the living is easy unless you're a pitcher. And it ends in the chill of fall, when gloves and bats and balls are ready for hibernation. The fields of play turn brown and harden, the snow falls. But to the eyes of the fan, already looking to next spring, the grass is ever green.

THE GAME FOR ALL AMERICA

The Fringe

Baseball is a horn of plenty for our people: an abundant provider of thrills and laughter and heroes and legends and, yes, prodigiously diverse livelihoods, too. Take my editor. Without baseball, he might have been forced to write steamy novels and lose sleep over his pyramid of tax shelters. Or the keyboard knights up in the pressbox, viewed with fear, if not loathing, by players and management alike. Baseball saved them the bother of extending their fireplace mantels to hold all those Oscars. Or the radio and television announcers, who without baseball would have had to report on four-star generals and five-alarm fires for the six o'clock news. Or the game's artists and photographers and trainers and general managers and publicity directors—baseball "saved" all of them from having to do something greater by the world's standards, but surely lesser by their own.

For what unites all of us on the fringe of the game—we who have made baseball our lives but are peripheral to its play—is an abiding love for the game, combined with Peter Pan's wish never to grow old, at least in our hearts. This is not to say that heedless infatuation plus arrested development is a surefire recipe for baseball success; only that, once again, Roy Campanella had it right: "You have to be a man," he said, "but you have to have a lot of little boy in you, too." It may be hard to think of Peter Ueberroth and George Steinbrenner in those terms, or Roger Angell or LeRoy Neiman or Vin Scully, but it is so.

And it is more evidently so as you move, to borrow Dudley Moore's marvelous phrase, beyond the fringe, into the lotus land where mild-mannered fans by day become fanatic figure filberts or demon microfilm readers by night. Dice baseball, the myriad computer baseball games, the search for the new statistic or the lost player—even fantasy baseball camps for the over-40 set. These all attest to the grip this great game has on America's heart and mind.

Card collectors, autograph hounds, broken-bat scavengers—the fringe widens to become in fact far larger than the core of players, spectators and workers at the stadium. The demarcation between stars and non-stars begins to blur, and this is as it should be, for baseball is about community, not clans—a ceremony of inclusion, not exclusion. As the title says, *The Game for All America*.

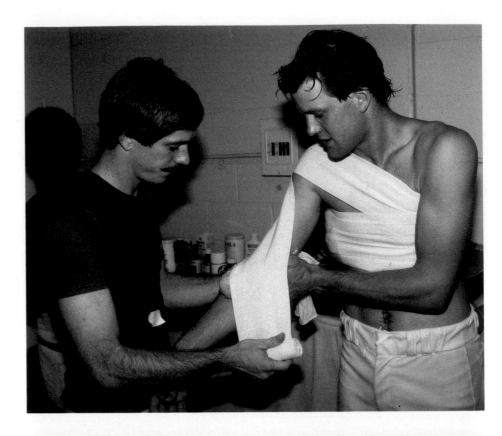

Somewhere between (or beyond) the toothy smile of Gary Carter and the wince of the sore-armed player in the trainer's room is the turkey-necked grimace of Max Patkin. Baseball's long-time clown prince is perhaps the last in a long line that stretches from the Browns' Arlie Latham a century ago on up through Germany Schaefer, Nick Altrock and Al Schacht. In recent years Bill Lee and Jay Johnstone have had their moments, but their humor was more hip and certainly less physical. Patkin knows he looks funny, and accentuates his farcical features with gyrations that have amused and astounded baseball fans for more than 40 years, since his days as a first-base coach for the Cleveland Indians and later St. Louis Browns. His employer both times? You guessed it—that master showman and ombudsman for ball park fun, Bill Veeck.

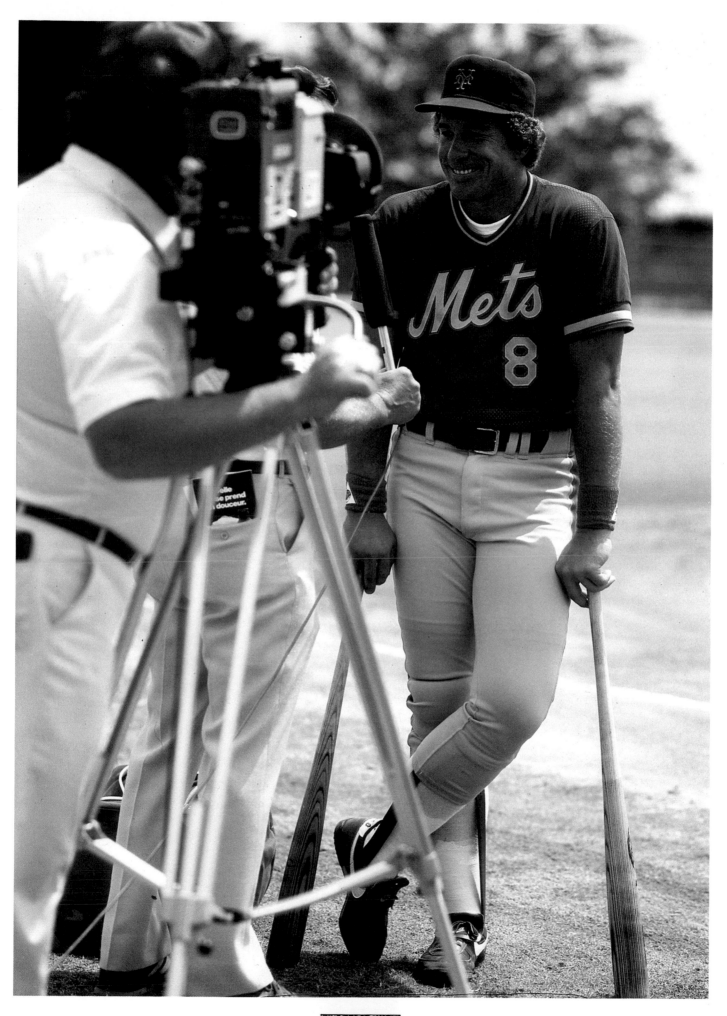

Baseball is not all glamour and excitement. For players and managers, those hours before and after the game do stretch on . . . and on. Filled with talk of hanging curveballs and hitting slumps or idle rumination about the mystery of it all, baseball's less-than-prime time affords its lesser lights the chance to shine. Writers and electronic-media types create the landscape across which our heroes stride; without chroniclers of their feats, who would remember them? If we know the names of Ajax and Hector, thousands of years after their deeds of valor, it is thanks to Homer, not to them. All hail the lowly scribe!

THE GAME FOR ALL AMERICA

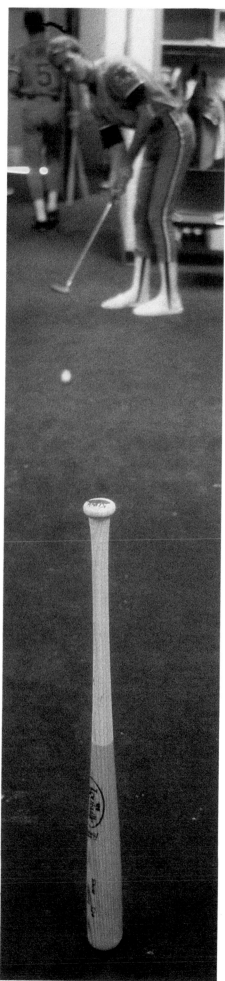

THE GAME FOR ALL AMERICA

Words and numbers and pictures are the imperishable remains of games played yesterday or long ago. Not even the sharpest eyes can detect all the things that transpire at a ball game, nor can the sharpest memory retain them. That's why every game, no matter how inconsequential, has its scorekeeper; why LeRoy Neiman sketches Dale Murphy; and why photographers doggedly pursue that perfect image.

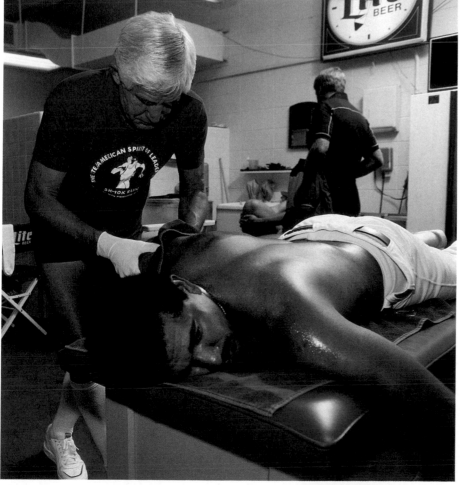

On the fringe of a baseball team gather the local reporters and photographers, but at World Series time that fringe swells to flood proportions as hundreds of press representatives from distant parts descend upon the scene. And what better illustration of baseball beyond the fringe than a canine wearing a Cincinnati Reds cap? The dog is Schottzie; the owner of the dog and the team whose cap he sports is Marge Schott. Like Max Patkin, Schottzie is part of a century-old tradition, highlighted by such luminaries as the Oakland A's mule Charley O., the Mets' basset hound Homer, and Fly and Prince, the greyhound mascots of the champion St. Louis Browns of the 1880s.

Clubhouse time is baseball's perpetual slow motion. Here, clean-up time at Denver's Mile High Stadium; bulk-up time at Dodger Stadium; line-up time at Reading's Municipal Stadium; and sum-up time at Anaheim.

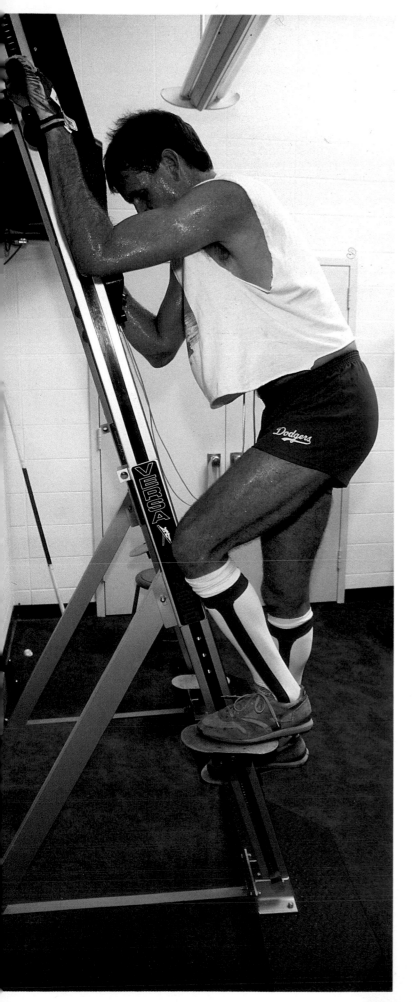

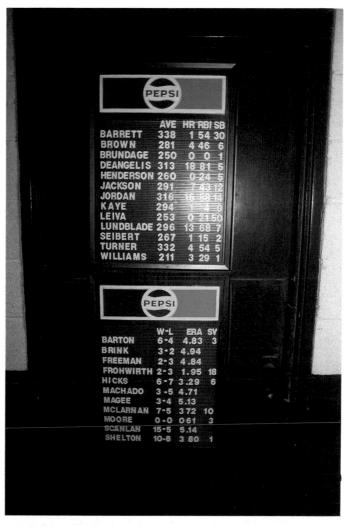

PEPSI

	AVE	HR	RBI	SB
BARRETT	338	1	54	30
BROWN	281	4	46	6
BRUNDAGE	250	0	0	1
DEANGELIS	313	18	81	5
HENDERSON	260	0	24	5
JACKSON	291	7	43	12
JORDAN	316	10	88	14
KAYE	294	1	4	0
LEIVA	253	0	21	50
LUNDBLADE	296	13	68	7
SEIBERT	267	1	15	2
TURNER	332	4	54	5
WILLIAMS	211	3	29	1

PEPSI

	W-L	ERA	SV
BARTON	6-4	4.83	3
BRINK	3-2	4.94	
FREEMAN	2-3	4.84	
FROHWIRTH	2-3	1.95	18
HICKS	6-7	3.29	6
MACHADO	3-5	4.71	
MAGEE	3-4	5.13	
MCLARNAN	7-5	372	10
MOORE	0-0	061	3
SCANLAN	15-5	5.14	
SHELTON	10-8	3 80	1

Has any human activity been so copiously recorded as baseball? That pitcher icing his arm knows his every action on the field is calibrated by some stat, captured by some photographer, commented on by some announcer or writer. But does he know—or by this point in his career, care—that even the clubhouse provides no sanctuary? A public life offers ample rewards, but it's a high-wire act without a net—every slip is in full view.

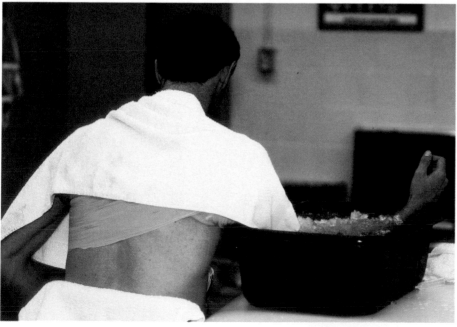

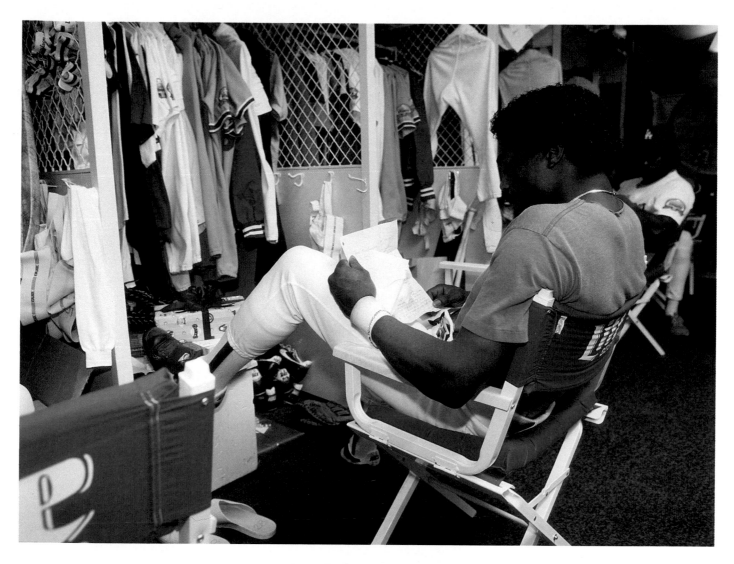

Read all about it! Baseball's the word, whether in the clubhouse area of the Salt Lake City Trappers, primed for a visit by the Pocatello Giants, or in the clubhouse of the Los Angeles Dodgers, trudging through a season of transition. Yes, baseball's the word, and cameraperson is one of the newer words in baseball. While women have not yet stormed the barricade of major league play, their talents are evident in every other area of the game, from front office to pressbox, from umpire to club president.

Baseball has been a vehicle for merchandising since at least the 1870s, when scorecard publishers sold advertising to local restaurants, sporting goods emporiums, railway companies and brewers. Today baseball sells cars, clothing, cameras, computers—anything and everything. It's smart business, companies all over the world have found, to identify your product with the game America loves. On the facing page, Lee Thomas of the Cardinals' front office handles prospect Perez gingerly—that's a kid's whole life in his hands. Indeed, there are 180 lives in the balance on the Cardinals' organizational board, whether they have the momentary security of a place on the 40-man roster or the frustrations of farm-team ball in Savannah or Johnson City.

ADMITTANCE by
PRESS PASS
ONLY

THE GAME FOR ALL AMERICA

Talkin' baseball. You don't have to be a pro, like Harry Caray or Joe Garagiola or Sparky Anderson, to expostulate on the finer points of the national pastime. Baseball is a great democratizer, the common tongue of all generations and social classes. As it is a principle of common law that a pauper may look upon a king, a fan may talk baseball with the conviction—and often as not, prowess—of a pro.

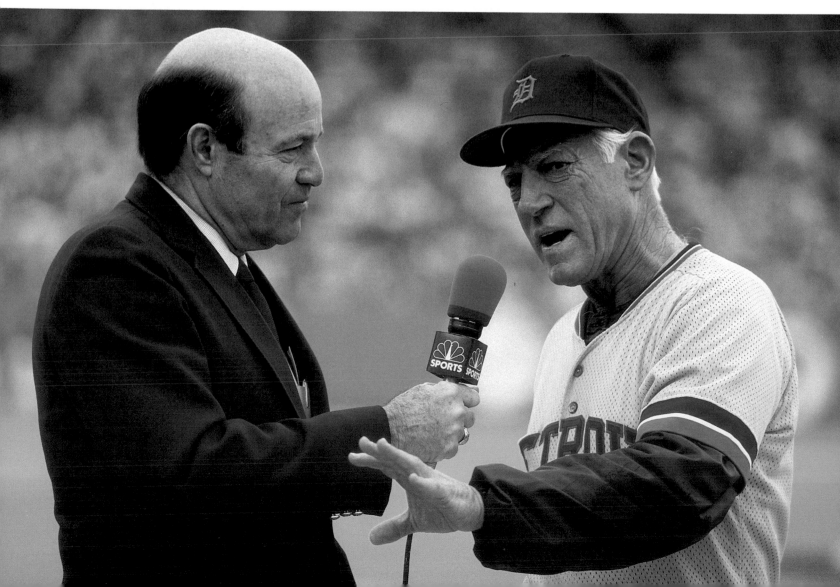

Baseball and show business have long been closely allied and, since the dawn of the television age, have become perhaps one and the same thing. Tommy Lasorda's rapport with Frank Sinatra and other screen stars was prefigured by John McGraw's friendship with George M. Cohan and his membership in the Lambs Club. Many baseball players have crossed from the baselines to the boards—among them Mike Donlin, Chuck Connors, John Berardino, Rube Marquard, Frank Chance, Babe Ruth and Cap Anson. How close are baseball and the stage? A century ago, when the New York Giants were the darlings of the Broadway set, actor and rabid fan DeWolf Hopper went so far as to incorporate baseball gags into his light-operatic parts. On August 14, 1888, he invited Anson's White Stockings and Jim Mutrie's Giants to a performance of "Prince Methusalem," and during the second act recited for them a previously unheard ballad called "Casey at the Bat."

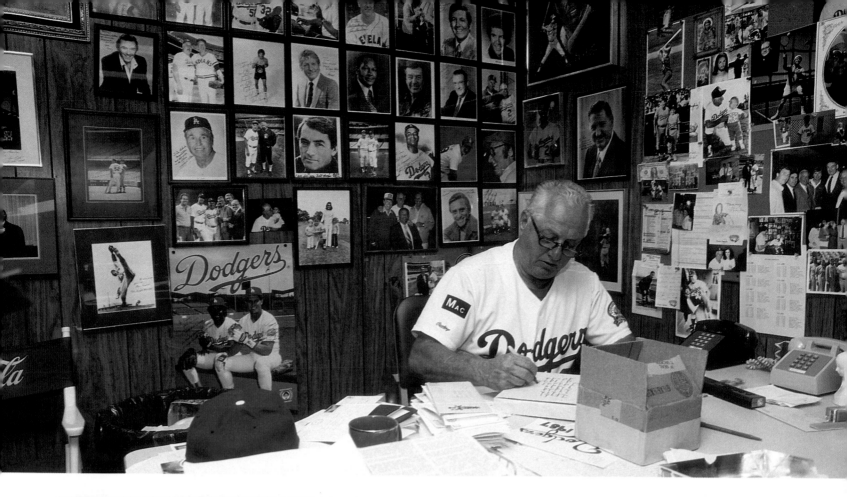

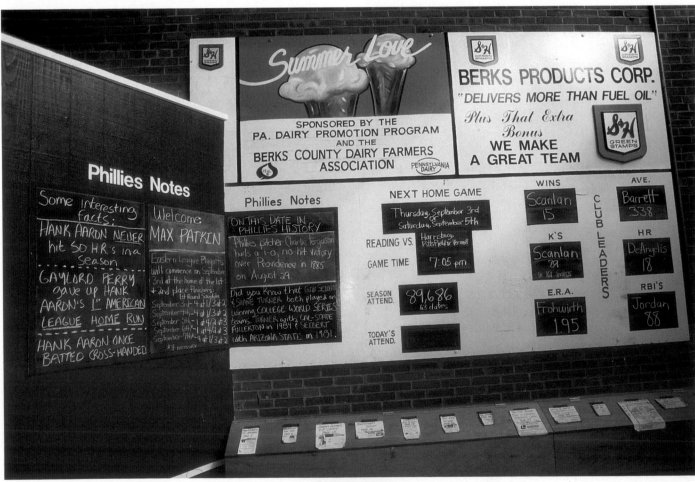

THE GAME FOR ALL AMERICA

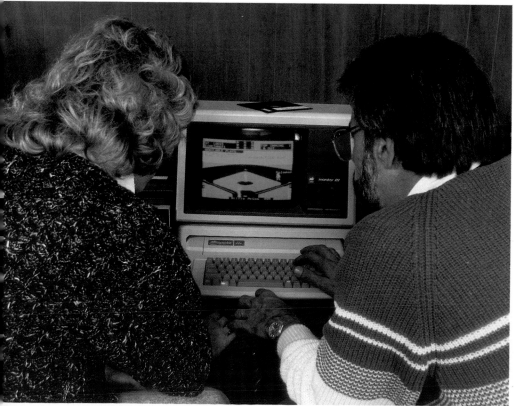

In baseball lingo until the 1980s, a cursor movement described an umpire's ejection of an offending player. Now, for the countless devotees of computerized fantasy baseball, first base has become part of a data base and a hard drive doesn't carry to the warning track. And yet baseball lives as much in the past as the present and future. A visitor to Vero Beach, Fla., and Dodgertown will know who the streets are named for. The locker room of the San Antonio Dodgers is not notably different from a locker room of half a century ago. And the Reading management presumes that its fans will connect with the exploits of a Phillie forebear on August 29, 1885. America's grand old game is made up of a million pieces, indivisible, with gaiety and triumph for all.

The Game

We grow up in baseball, and we grow old with it. In between we go through some changes, but the game is a fixed point; it is always there for us, like religion, like family—even if for a time we turn aside from it to get on with "real life." Surely many of us never knew how much we loved this game until we had children to share it with, to teach its ways, tell its stories and glory in its heroes.

Baseball gives us models, values and mementos to pass on. For America's sons and daughters, a Babe Ruth or Ozzie Smith is a member of the family—more so than distant relatives who are seldom seen and whose deeds are unrecorded. A hero can be just like a cousin in the Navy whose far-flung adventures we admire and personalize. "I saw Mike Schmidt when he first came up," a Phillies fan might say knowingly, though perhaps aided by 20-20 hindsight, "and even though he hit only .196 that first year, I could tell he was going to be a great one." In this way Schmidt's 500 homers become the fan's, and make him heroic, too.

I remember how my whole being quivered when, as a boy of 10, I tore through the morning newspaper to get to the sports pages. The Dodgers scored three in the bottom of the ninth and Duke Snider hit two homers? I couldn't have been prouder had I hit them myself.

Yet in the end, in the long season that describes American life, what survives is not players or fans, not even the concrete-and-steel stadiums, simply the game. The game is the constant, itself taking on the shape of family as new players and new fans, bolstered by the lore of those who preceded them, come on to replace the old.

There is a special poignance to the passage of time in baseball. As all clocks are stopped in the confines of the ball park, where the game ain't over till it's over, so is the fan impervious to the slipping sands of time. The heroes of our youth grow old, yet we seem the same. That's why such occasions as Old Timers' Day or the Hall of Fame induction ceremonies are so sadly sweet; better, we may think for a moment, to preserve these heroes in our memories as they were, frozen in a baseball-card pose, so that we too might stay young forever.

But no . . . the power and the glory of the game reside in its blurring of past and present, its promise of endless summer.

The impulse is strong: take a good lead, get a jump on the next base. Yet the instinct of caution (or perhaps the rule of this boy's league) keeps one foot planted on the base. How much this picture says about growing up!

The green fields of Fenway are ever the same, the action ever different. When Boston's Jim Rice flips second basemen or shortstops, they know they've been flipped—but hey, they're major leaguers, too, and more often than not complete their own balletic flip to first. Umpires take it all in, with scarcely a moment's respite; what relief they get comes in small doses.

Oddibe young again, now that springtime is here! The smiles of a sunny day are not confined to the Texas Rangers' Oddibe McDowell—they abound at ball parks across America, where a line of bats can take on a robotized sort of life, like Mickey Mouse's brooms in *The Sorcerer's Apprentice,* or T-ballers can approach a baseball with a toreador's blend of bravado and self-defense.

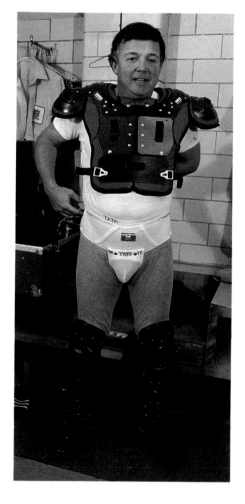

One of the socially useful lessons the game teaches is acquiescence to authority. If the ump says you're out, it doesn't matter that you were safe; you're out. The question, "What's under an umpire's uniform?" may not have the enduring fascination of "What's under a Scotsman's kilt?", but at least it has an answer, as supplied here by National League ump Terry Tata. The determinedly scruffy Little League ump above belies the adage that clothing makes the man.

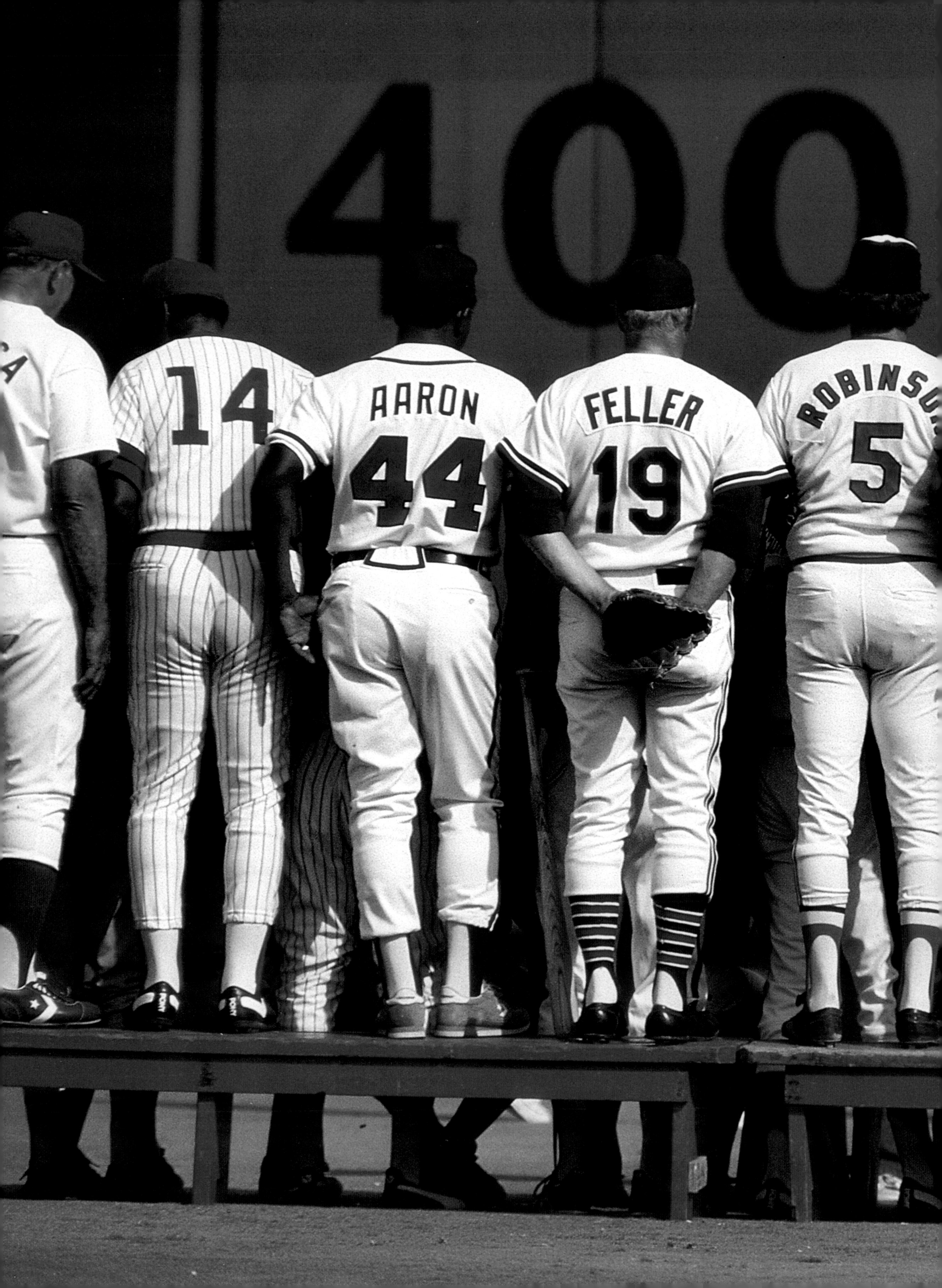
400
14
AARON
44
FELLER
19
5

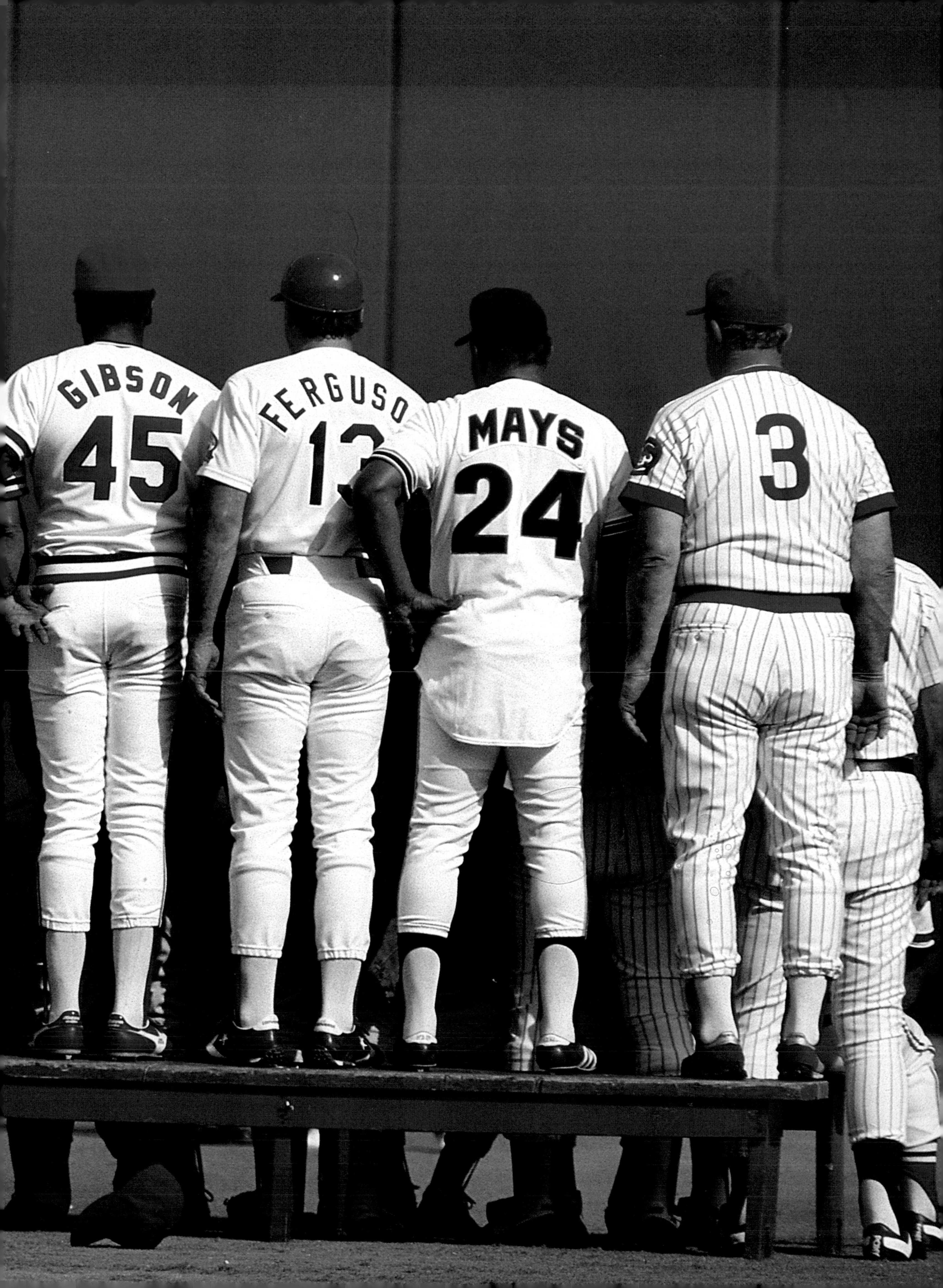
GIBSON
45
FERGUSO
13
MAYS
24
3

(Pages 218-219)
Note the "400" marker before which this dream team is posed. When most of these stars broke in, that number represented the elite in blue-blood society and in baseball, where it was the sum of the major league rosters—16 teams, 25 men per. How would a team comprised of these men in their primes fare over a full season today? Or in the age of Cobb and Wagner? It is a fan's ultimate fantasy.

So many magnificent images occur on the ball field every day that the seasoned eye no longer sees half of them. Yet take a Briton to a baseball game and while he will dutifully compliment the speed of our hurlers and the power of our batsmen, his praise for our fielders will border on the ecstatic. Even what seem to us to be fairly routine defensive efforts, like Shawon Dunston's spring-training leap over the Rangers' Darrell Porter, is to the rest of the world miraculous. Food for thought—unlike the San Diego Chicken, who provides (or rather, embodies) food for fun.

Some of us bridled at the forced recitation of the Pledge of Allegiance in grade school; others balked at the hierarchy and ritual of the church or temple; still others rebelled against what they saw as an increasingly intrusive and impersonal government. Yet place all these nonconformists in a ball park, strike up a few bars of *The Star Spangled Banner*, and patriotism is palpable in the air.

Did you hear the one about the kid who was wandering around downtown St. Louis in a baseball uniform when he stopped a passer-by to ask, "How do I get to Busch Stadium?" The reply, of course: "Practice, practice."

Game time approaches. Players wander onto the field for the American Legion World Series, members of the Maine Guides stroll beneath the grandstand at Old Orchard Beach, and Iron Mike has his line of baseballs ready for duty.

Getting it right is a frustrating goal. Just when you thought you'd conquered that changeup, just when you thought you could get it over anytime you wanted . . . mastery slips away. In baseball the quest for self-improvement never ends, and the Kansas City Royals find that it helps to have inspirational surroundings.

The wide world can be a confusing place, where clouds of ambivalence swirl around every choice. The imperatives in baseball, on the other hand, are blissfully clear: either you do or you don't. The Little League strikeout victim didn't, the catcher

did; A's catcher Terry Steinbach
didn't, Minnesota baserunner Al
Newman did. In baseball's
beautiful but harsh symmetry,
every player's success is
simultaneously balanced by
another's failure.

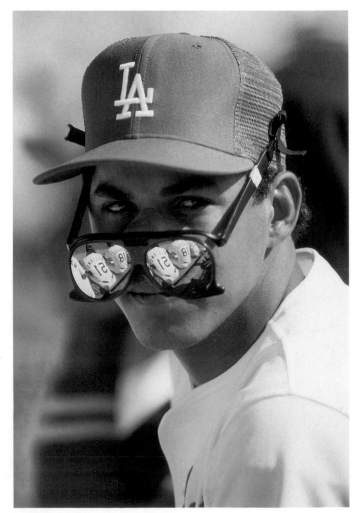

It's a nice feeling to be one of the gang. When you're part of a team, whether it's an All-Star aggregate like the National Leaguers below or a Little League nine, you become the equal—in stature if not in ability—of the team's best player. Baseball celebrates the virtues of team play and camaraderie, but fundamentally it is a game of and for individuals. Although it is contested by two teams, at almost every point of the action the game pits one man against nine. As a team structure that permits and encourages maximum individual performance and expression (to the point of sacrilege, such as the shelving of Dodger Blue on St. Pat's Day), baseball is a model democratic institution and truly a game for America.

How far will this Little Leaguer go in baseball? Impossible to say, and hardly a question he should be burdened with now. In 1953 Joey Jay, age 17, became the first graduate of the Little League program to enter the major leagues. Like so many exceptional baseball prospects under the age of 12, Jay pitched and batted third. As he went on in baseball, his pitching talent blossomed but his hitting leveled off. What's amazing, when you think of it, is that in this century only one man has been able to retain that boyhood dominance of mound and plate all the way up to the majors—the singular Babe Ruth.

Unlike football, that sublimated form of war which sneers at snow and sleet and trudges on, baseball is a game in harmony with the elements, deferring to their more forceful protestations against play. But no game has ever been called on account of sun. Baseball players have to stand up to Old Sol, or improvise solutions.

Bat-and-ball games began in ancient Egypt as a form of fertility ritual and sun worship. On this page three major leaguers hearken back to baseball's desert days: (clockwise from top left) Alfredo Griffin, Jose Guzman and Dave Righetti. Opposite is Joe Cowley, whose experience in 1987 could aptly be termed a hatful of rain. After winning 11 games for the White Sox in 1986, including a no-hitter, he was traded to Philadelphia. There, in the sudden and inexplicable manner of Steve Blass and Kevin Saucier before him, he lost home plate and his career. In 11 2/3 calamitous innings as a Phillie he allowed 21 hits, 17 walks and 26 runs, and called it quits.

You're out of here! Man in blue Tom Hallion turns crimson, tossing the offending party *con brio*. On the facing page, an arbiter bakes on both sides as he takes abuse from the visiting Iowa Cubs and the Louisville Cardinal fans. And the Little League umpire shows that while his colleagues know how to take the heat and how to dish it out, he knows how to keep his cool.

THE GAME FOR ALL AMERICA

Play ball means something more than runs
Or pitches thudding into gloves!
Remember through the summer suns
This is the game your country loves.
　　　　　　　　　—Grantland Rice

The skull sessions under the spreading oak and the grounders scooped in pregame drills prove their purpose in the heat of competition. It's a long road from Little League to major league, and there are plenty of forks in the road beyond. Look at Mike Scott of the Astros, who hit the big time with a thud as a New York Met and only four years later attained stardom. And so the game offers up yet another life lesson: If at first you don't succeed. . . .

Ready, set, go! The camera catches the Yankees' Don Mattingly and the Angels' Mark McLemore listening for the starter's pistol, and Toronto's Tony Fernandez in an improbable pushup. The closeup of Bert Blyleven's fastball grip recalls Jim Bouton's conclusion to *Ball Four:* "You spend a good piece of your life gripping a baseball and in the end it turns out that it was the other way around all the time."

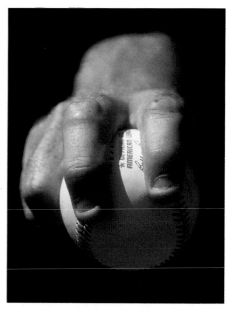

"Baseball-American," Ring Lardner called the invasion of the game's argot into the nation's language. On these pages we see some Baseball-American origins. Double play, rhubarb, hit-and-run, caught off base. Add to these such vernacular phrases as ball-park figure, rabbit ears, raincheck, screwball, benchwarmer, bush leaguer, and scores more. All are baseball terms and images, of course, but think how impoverished the language of citizens unconcerned with baseball—if such Americans exist—would be without them.

The beauty of baseball is in small things—a Renoir-like still life on a
Little League bench, a small hand clasped by a hero's larger one, a
catcher's sign blazing secretly in the sun. And the joy is in the athleticism
of a skirmish at second base (here, the Dodgers' Steve Sax is taken out by
the Mets' Keith Miller) or a little guy (here the Pirates' John Cangelosi)
hitting a home run.

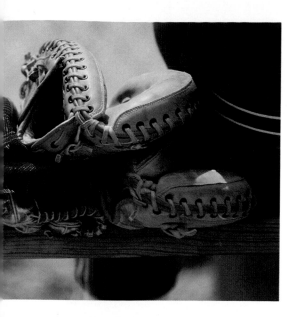
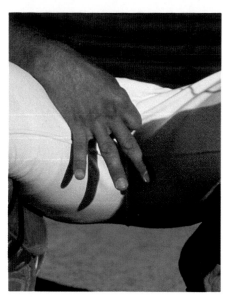

Read Benito Santiago's lips: Be it ever so dusty, there's no place like home. Home is where the run is, and games are won with runs. A close play at second base or third is thrilling, but nothing in baseball compares with the tableau of runner, ball and catcher intersecting at the plate. And in the end, isn't coming home what baseball is all about?